"In this heartfelt, clear, and c [obscured] us the importance of welcon [obscured] ...as welcomed us. Through biblical insight, lived experience, and encouraging stories of her dear friends welcoming people in many different contexts, Jen gives the reader space to contemplate the importance of being a welcoming people and a welcoming church, not only on a Sunday but every day, and not only for the growth of your church but for the growth of the kingdom worldwide. This is a book that I want to put into the hands of every member of my church."

STEVE ROBINSON, Senior Pastor, Cornerstone Church Liverpool, UK; Director, Acts 29 Great Britain

"The most welcoming place on the planet should be the church, and the most welcoming people on the planet should be Christians. Why? So that sinners can hear the good news of the gospel of Jesus Christ. In *Welcome*, we are invited to fling open the doors of the church and open the doors of our lives so that all people will have the chance to hear about who Jesus is and what he has accomplished for a lost and dying world."

J.T. ENGLISH, Lead Pastor, Storyline Fellowship, Arvada, Colorado; Author, *Deep Discipleship: How the Church Can Make Whole Disciples of Jesus*

"Jen offers theological reasons and practical action steps for churches and individuals wanting to practice the radical welcome of Jesus on a regular basis in their local church community. This book will encourage and equip you to see yourself as a partner with God in his kingdom work—on Sundays and beyond!"

AMY GANNETT, Author, *Fix Your Eyes: How Our Study of God Shapes Our Worship of Him*

"*Welcome* provides biblical encouragement to mirror the work of our kind and hospitable God. Jen Oshman encourages readers to sacrificially welcome others as Christ welcomed us. I want to give every member of my local church a copy of this compelling book!"

HUNTER BELESS, Host, Journeywomen Podcast; Author, *Read It, See It, Say It, Sing It!*

"The gospel should create a culture of welcome (Romans 15:7) so that the local church is, as Jen Oshman beautifully puts it, 'a porch light in a dark night.' This is all the more important in a time of deep loneliness and fragmentation. This wonderful book will help both church leaders and regular members build a culture in their churches that reflects the welcome of the gospel. It is filled with practical ideas, biblical and historical wisdom, and counsel that touches the heart. Highly recommended!"

GAVIN ORTLUND, Pastor, First Baptist Church of Ojai, California; Author, *Why God Makes Sense in a World That Doesn't*

"Those who have experienced God's extravagant welcome in Christ should be obsessed with sharing it as widely and generously as we can. Yet it is easy to be inward-focused, comfortable in our church communities, and blind to the needs of our neighbours—and to the barriers that get in the way of them joining us. Jen Oshman draws on the Scriptures and her own experiences of church-planting and cross-cultural missions to show how our churches can be places of welcome and belonging for everyone. Written with warmth and wisdom, this book will inspire and equip individuals and church families to reflect the welcome of our Saviour."

CAROLYN LACEY, Women's Worker, Woodgreen Church, Worcester, UK; Author, *Extraordinary Hospitality (for Ordinary People)*

"Quality welcome, quality teaching, and quality hospitality are three key ingredients of a flourishing church. Jen highlights the two of these that all Christians need to reflect in their personal lives if the body of Christ is to demonstrate his grace. She reminds us that the God who has welcomed us—welcomed you!—can use us to welcome others. What a privilege that is. How significant that is! So, read this book and absorb some of Jen's lovely insights."

RAY EVANS, FIEC Leadership Consultant, and formerly Lead Pastor at Grace Community Church, Bedford, UK

welcome

JEN OSHMAN

Welcome:
Loving Your Church by Making Space for Everyone
© 2023 Jen Oshman

Published by:
The Good Book Company

thegoodbook.com | thegoodbook.co.uk
thegoodbook.com.au | thegoodbook.co.nz | thegoodbook.co.in

Cover design by Faceout Studio | Art direction and design by André Parker

ISBN: 9781784988289 | Printed in the UK

For Redemption Parker
You welcome so well

CONTENTS

FOREWORD

BY TIM CHALLIES

Of all the tasks that may fall to me on a Sunday morning, my favorite is to stand by the doors of the church, greet people as they arrive, and welcome them to our worship service. I'm not the most outgoing person in the world, so it's not like this comes naturally. I'm not the most loquacious person in the world, so it's not like the words flow easily. But it has still become my favorite task because I believe in it so deeply.

As I stand there, I have the privilege of greeting people who are very much like me and people who are very different. I welcome those who are young and those who are old, those who have served Christ for decades and those who have known him for only a week. I welcome those who are dear friends and those I have never met, those who have resided in my country for their entire lives and those who have only just arrived. I welcome the strong and the weak, the happy and the sad, the well-known and the anonymous, the believer and the unbeliever. And I welcome them all to join in the same activity in the same place and for the same purpose. There's something so sweetly unifying about it, something so deeply moving.

That simple welcome is not merely a means to usher people from the front door to their seat. Its value is not merely practical. Rather, it is a picture—a picture of something much greater, a symbol of something much more precious. In its own way, that welcome represents God's welcome to those he loves. As I welcome people to Grace Fellowship Church, I am reminding them of the way God welcomes them into his kingdom. As I welcome people to this brief time of worship, I am reminding them that God welcomes them into an eternity of worship. Isn't it so often true of God's ways that something that appears so small can actually mean so much?

In this short but meaty book—one that mines deep truths from Scripture and then applies them in very practical ways—Jen Oshman wants you to consider that because God has welcomed you, it falls to you to welcome others. Not only that, but in the way God has welcomed you, he now calls you to welcome them. The God who has related to you with such kindness, such generosity, such magnanimity now calls you to relate to others likewise.

Of course this goes far beyond taking your post at the front doors of the church for 30 minutes on the occasional Sunday morning. It extends to what happens before the service but also during and after it. It extends to how you behave in the church but also to how you behave in the home and neighborhood. It directs the way you relate to friends but also to strangers and even enemies. It impacts your hospitality and your evangelism, your weekdays as much as your weekends.

It turns out that a true welcome is not just a hand extended on a Sunday morning but a way to live the Christian life. I'm thankful for this book and gladly commend it to you. May you read it and then prayerfully consider how to do it—how to welcome others with all the joy, all the devotion, with which God has welcomed you.

Tim Challies
Blogger and author;
Elder, Grace Fellowship Church, Toronto
August 2022

INTRODUCTION

I remember being on a mission trip years ago and chatting with another woman on the team as we waited to board our plane from Japan to Thailand. We were living in Japan at the time, ministering to the American military stationed there. The mission team was made up of men and women from all military branches and ranks—everything from a newly enlisted Marine up to a high-ranking Air Force officer, and a wide variety in between.

My friend and teammate Jenna remarked, "We have a pretty weird team here. I can't imagine seeing a group of people like this anywhere else." And she was right. Not only did the team members come from all branches and ranks, but they hailed from all over the United States and represented a number of ethnicities. What we felt even more, though, was the diversity in personalities. As members of the same church family, we not only met every weekend for worship, but we had been participating in various team-building activities and planning meetings for months. We all knew each other well at this point. And, I'll be honest, some people were easier to be around than others.

This truth was veiled in Jenna's comment. She didn't say it out loud, but we gave one another knowing looks and stifled a giggle. Our team included some tough and sometimes unpredictable personalities. Melding together strong people from so many backgrounds was indeed a wonder.

My husband, who was sitting a chair or two away from us, picked up on our conversation. He said with a knowing grin, "Yeah. You don't get to pick your family, do you?"

We both smiled and sighed and shook our heads. "No, you sure don't," Jenna said.

My own family flooded my thoughts. I have some crazy cousins, let me tell you. My aunts and uncles all live very different lives, spread out all over the United States. My own brother and I couldn't be more different. Our dad was an only child from a quiet family, and our mom is the oldest of five, and we have more than 30 cousins on her side. People in my family are all over the place when it comes to personalities, strengths, joys, sorrows, work ethic, values, and demeanor.

And it's true, I didn't choose this family. You could say it chose me. Or more accurately, God himself chose it for me. In his goodness and providence, he ordained that I would share my blood, family tree, dysfunction, and celebrations with these people. We don't get to pick our family.

This is true of our church family too. We Christians don't choose each other. We didn't even choose Christ; he chose us. And he made us forever part of his people, on earth and in heaven. We are siblings in the global Christian family, joined together by the Son, indwelt by the Spirit, and under the sovereign goodness of the Father.

Our global faith family is made up of millions of local faith families—local churches. As you think about your own local church, I imagine you have feelings similar to those described above; some members of the family are easier to be around than others. You find some members so like-minded that it's natural and just plain fun to be with them. Others view the world in ways so different from you that you are tempted to dismiss them or at least avoid them. This much is sure: you don't select the people who join your local church—God does that. And he makes a family that is at times delightful, and at other times requires patience and tenacity and trust that God really does know what he's doing. Our local faith families are beautiful and good and hard and quirky and stretching and everything in between.

And this crazy, beautiful family that you and I are in is all because of one thing: the radical welcome of Jesus. Because of the Father's great love and endless mercy, he sacrificed his own Son to welcome us in. In Christ's death and resurrection, you and I are reconciled, made new, and made family. We are adopted sons and daughters, heirs together in Christ. Jesus stopped at nothing to welcome us into the family.

And he says to you and me: *Go and do likewise.*

As we have been welcomed, so we must welcome. Our God, who made space for you and me, asks us to make space for everyone, so that they can hear and respond to his good news.

Yet that's not always easy, is it? While you may love your church family fiercely, welcoming outsiders in can sometimes feel awkward and daunting. Church feels outdated and irrelevant to so many. In the post-Christian West, we who attend worship services on Sundays are not the norm. It is nothing short of a leap of faith to invite an outsider into your local church. If you bring a friend to church, you wonder how they will be welcomed in. Will anyone even talk to them? Or will they be ignored or quietly sidelined because they don't fit in? Will they find church to be what so many of those outside of it suspect it of being: stuffy or cliquey or cold?

May it never be. Jesus *really* is the way, the truth, and the life. His Word *really* is the word of life. And the church *really* is God's plan for imparting healing and goodness and beauty to the world. Brothers and sisters, we have an opportunity now to be a porch light in a dark night. The brokenness of the world swirls around us. So many on our streets and in our workplaces are suffering: buckling under the weight of sickness or broken relationships or unmet expectations, just trying to make sense of it all. We long to love them and serve them and help them.

But how? How might we welcome the people of our communities into our church services and ultimately into the very family of God? How might we put the always-needed, eternally relevant, forever-glorious love of Jesus on display so that others might be brought in? How can we make space for everyone?

As you turn the pages of this book and turn to your Father in prayer, he will show you. God is our help. He turns the fatherless into sons and daughters. So put your hope in Jesus. Believe in the help and pursuit of the Holy Spirit. Trust in the goodness of the Father.

It's true, we don't choose our faith family. Our God does that. And he will. As he welcomed you, so he will empower you to welcome others.

1. HOW JESUS
WELCOMES US

Ten years ago, our family made a global move. We had been living in Okinawa, Japan for nearly a decade, where my husband pastored a church for American military personnel and their families. We believed, though, that God had called us to the city of Brno in the Czech Republic, one of the world's most atheist nations. So, along with our Asian-raised daughters, who were aged 16, 10, 8, and 6, and our Japanese chocolate Labrador Retriever, we moved 9,000 miles from the tropics in the East China Sea to the gray winter of Central Europe just ten days before Christmas.

Everything about our first Sunday in our new Czech church was as foreign to us as the language. Not only could we not speak a word of Czech—the Slavic language employs sounds the English speaker has never heard nor formed—but we didn't yet know a soul. We went from being the pastor's family on the inside of the church to being total newcomers nervously standing on the outside of the church. We needed our new brothers and sisters to show us everything, like when to sit and when to stand during the service, how to take communion according to their tradition, and how to pronounce their names over coffee after church. We were totally at their mercy as we sought to make this new church, new country, and new faith family our home.

Today's global economy and increasingly transient lifestyles mean that you may well have made a few moves yourself. Even if you haven't moved a great distance, it's not unusual to have moved from one church to another at some point. And the fact that you're reading this book means there was a day when you walked through the front doors of your current church venue for the very first time.

Can you remember what it was like? Palms a little sweaty, breathing a little faster, heart thumping a little bit harder? Most first-time visitors feel this way. Questions flood our minds as we walk into the sanctuary. What if everyone else talks to one another but not to me? What if I sit down or raise my hand or say, "Amen" at the wrong time and everyone shifts in their pews to stare at me? Visiting a new church requires courage.

And how much more courage is required for those who are not yet followers of Christ? While our first Sunday in the Czech church was trying, we knew we were already among family. But there was an occasion, years prior, when I entered the doors of a church as someone who did not yet know or love Jesus. My mom, who was a single mother, took me to church for the first time when I was nine years old. I could tell right away that we were different from the families gathered there. Sure, I knew the language being spoken, but I had no idea what we were getting ourselves into. That church was perhaps even more foreign to me then than the one I encountered in Brno years later.

For those who are not yet Christians, exploring the Christian faith and way of life requires a certain desperation, or at least a determination, to make it through the church front door. The question, then, for those of us on the inside is: How might we cross the wide divide to meet those who are on the outside? How might we become a people of welcome—a people who make complete strangers feel that they can come in and be right at home? How can we create an atmosphere that invites our neighbors who are strangers to become our brothers and sisters in Jesus, as they repent and believe the good news?

If we want to welcome others into Jesus' family, we need to start by looking at Jesus himself.

THE SELF-SACRIFICING WELCOME OF JESUS

Jesus displayed his heart of welcome when he set out on a rescue mission 2,000 years ago. What a distance Jesus traveled—what an incomprehensible divide he crossed—in pursuit of you and me. He traded in his throne for a manger, his kingly majesty for skin and a frail body and the transcendence of heaven for the tangibility of walking this earth—so that humans might see him, touch him, and believe in him.

Still he went further. May it be ever fresh in our minds that while we were enemies of God, Jesus gave himself over to a violent death so that we might be reconciled to the Father (Romans 5:10). It's easy to get so cozy in our Christianity that we forget we were spiritually dead, following the ways of the world, when God, because of his great love and mercy, "made us alive with Christ" (Ephesians 2:1-5). We are Christians through no effort of our own. It's only because of the kindness and compassion of our Lord that we've been welcomed into his family.

This is the greatest scandal in history. No greater divide has ever been crossed in history. No one has ever traveled farther or suffered more to welcome their enemies in. Jesus, the Creator and God of the universe, exchanged all the goodness of heaven and *joyfully* endured the cross (Hebrews 12:2) so that you and I might become children of God (John 1:12).

FOLLOWING AFTER JESUS
With God's help and the leading of his Spirit, we can follow after Jesus and warmly welcome others as they become part of our faith families. That's what Paul calls the believers in Philippi to as he describes Jesus's downward journey in Philippians 2:5-11:

⁵ In your relationships with one another, have the same mindset as Christ Jesus: ⁶ Who, being in very nature God, did not consider equality with God something to be used to his own advantage; ⁷ rather, he made himself nothing by taking the very nature of a servant, being made in human likeness. ⁸ And being found in appearance as a man, he humbled himself by becoming obedient to death—even death on a cross! ⁹ Therefore God exalted him to the highest place and gave him the name that is above every name, ¹⁰ that at the name of Jesus every knee should bow, in heaven and on earth and under the earth, ¹¹ and every tongue acknowledge that Jesus Christ is Lord, to the glory of God the Father.

Paul instructs us to have the mind of Jesus and empty ourselves out. We follow Jesus by forsaking our status, becoming servants, and fully humbling ourselves.

Forsake Your Status

Jesus is God. Before the incarnation, as one Person of the Trinity, God the Son's status was as King over all, worthy of all majesty and adoration (Philippians 2:6). But we see also that he did not grasp (ESV) or cling to (NLT) his status. He didn't exploit his position (CSB) or take advantage of his own nature (NIV).

We who belong to Christ also enjoy a privileged status. We are co-heirs with him (Romans 8:17) and have all the benefits of being God's adopted sons and daughters. And it can be easy to take advantage of our status as "insiders" without realizing it. Unless we are intentional about being otherwise, we easily get comfortable inside our own faith families and just stay put. I've heard this called a *holy huddle*—the saints gathered in an impenetrable circle with their backs to the outside world. This happens when we subconsciously look only to our own needs and don't have eyes to see those standing on the outside.

Kenton and Jaimie are a well-loved young couple at our church. Everyone wants to be in their small group because they are so good at building friendships and nurturing intimacy. But on Sunday mornings you will not find them cozied up inside a clique of friends. Even with their three young children tangled around their feet, they always make a beeline for newcomers. They make a concerted effort to introduce themselves to every visitor, and they always extend an invitation to their home. Week in and week out, Kenton and Jaimie forsake their status, leaving the comfort of their long-held and deep friendships, to ensure that every stranger receives a warm welcome.

Become a Servant

Second, in Jesus' immeasurably compassionate rescue mission, "he made himself nothing by taking the very nature of a servant, being made in human likeness" (Philippians 2:7). Though he is more powerful than anything or anyone else in all of creation, our God "did not come to be served, but to serve, and to give his life as a ransom for many" (Matthew 20:28). Jesus emptied himself (Philippians 2:7 CSB, ESV); he gave up his divine privileges (NLT); he made himself nothing (NIV)—that we might be welcomed into his family. And he calls his followers to do the same.

Let's be real: serving is hard. I think all of us would prefer to walk through the doors into church on Sunday and be handed a warm cup of coffee and sit down in a cushy chair to consume the worship service like a paying customer—much like going to the movies at one of those theaters with reclining chairs and bottomless soda and popcorn. The comparison is laughable—the church is not the movies! But do we who are members of the faith family approach our times together ready to empty ourselves out? Do we view our church gatherings as a place to receive or as a place to give?

Before my husband and I headed for the mission field, we were loved and discipled well by the staff and members of the church that married us and sent us out. I'll never forget one Sunday morning close to our departure. As was our usual custom when taking communion, the congregation arose and lined up to receive the bread and wine at the front of the sanctuary. Mark and I were in line, a few people behind the head pastor's wife. I watched her get out of line, take a few steps to the left, and bend down on one knee to scrape gum off the floor. Rather than ignore the mess or assume a janitor would tend to it later, she humbled herself and served the whole church family by instantly taking on this dirty job. That example inspired me as I left to share Christ overseas—and it continues to remind me now that I am not too good to empty myself out. As I follow Jesus, I am not above serving in any capacity—whatever it takes to create an atmosphere of welcome.

Humble Yourself unto Death

I know, things just got real. I realize the heading above this paragraph is startling and unsettling. *Unto death*? Well, yes. Jesus really did say, "Whoever wants to be my disciple must deny themselves and take up their cross and follow me" (Mark 8:34). As we progress through Philippians 2, we see that Jesus not only refused to take advantage of his status as God, and not only became a servant in human likeness, but he also "humbled himself by becoming obedient to death—even death on a cross!" (v 8).

Our Savior stopped at *nothing* to welcome us in.

Jesus' welcome is one of moving toward the outsider. He laid himself down. He cast aside his status and poured himself out. He gave everything—*his very life, which ended in a violent death*—to welcome us into the family. He does not stand far off, aloof, and cold. He does not require us to clean ourselves up before coming to him. He seeks us. He left heaven and came to us. Oh, what a merciful Savior! Oh, what an unfathomably good King!

Paul tells us to "have the same mindset as Christ Jesus" (Philippians 2:5). I don't know what this might look like in your own life and faith family, but I do know that

Jesus asks us to follow him. We may not be required to follow him to an early grave, but we are certainly called to put to death all the pride and selfishness that lurks in our hearts. Yet he is worthy of our following. Brothers and sisters, let us have the mind of Christ. By his spirit, he lives inside us, and he will help us. Let us empty ourselves, serve others, and obey our Lord as we go to great lengths to welcome the stranger into our Christian families.

GOD WILL GIVE US HEARTS OF WELCOME

"Forsake your status"; "become a servant"; "humble yourself". Perhaps, as you've read this chapter, you are weighed down by the burden of welcoming. If you're like me, you have looked back on your welcoming ways and found that you fall short. I know I have not welcomed others to the extent that God has welcomed me.

Let's take a deep sigh of relief and remember our God will help us. As we have seen, Jesus came down. He draws near. The Holy Spirit lives inside us and is ever ready to equip us with hearts of welcome. He does not require us to conjure them up in our own strength. When you and I joined the family of God, he said he "will give you a new heart and put a new spirit in you; I will remove from you your heart of stone and give you a heart of flesh. And I will put my Spirit in you and move you to follow my decrees and be careful to keep my laws" (Ezekiel 36:26-27). And what God promises he always delivers.

When our Czech brothers and sisters welcomed us that first Sunday in Brno, they did so out of the overflow of their hearts. They were patient with us because Jesus had been patient with them and his spirit lived inside them. Kenton and Jaimie have grown in their capacity for and commitment to welcoming others because the Holy Spirit in them has sanctified them, changed them, and helped them. My former pastor's wife was driven to love because she had first been loved (1 John 4:19). All of these Christ-followers were moved to follow his decrees because the Spirit in them moved them, just as the prophet Ezekiel says. And this truth applies to you and me too.

When we invite others in, it is because the Spirit in us has prompted us to do so. If you have a desire to be a welcoming follower of Jesus, praise God! That desire comes from him. Be encouraged. There is evidence of the Spirit's work in you. Cry out to him and ask him to continue to grow in you an open heart, which is bursting with hospitality and compassion and which results in open doors.

We are not left to our own devices, our own strength, or our own self-help. Jesus came down. We are his. Because he welcomed us and lives in us, we too can welcome.

ACTION STEPS
In light of Jesus' radical welcome of you and me, let us consider some ways in which we might grow in our desire and ability to warmly welcome others.

- *Imagine all that Jesus left behind when he came to rescue us and welcome us.* Remember that Jesus willingly laid aside the glory and comforts of heaven and chose to come to earth as a baby in a manger, born into an impoverished family. Remembering his great sacrifice for us spurs us to be willing to sacrifice for others too.

- *Study the many ways that Jesus poured himself out in the Gospels.* Consider reading through Matthew, Mark, Luke, and John over the next several months or whole year. Keep a notebook handy and jot down every time you read about Jesus emptying himself for the sake of others.

- *Reflect on how others have embodied a Philippians-2 attitude when welcoming you.* When have others forsaken themselves, become servants, and humbled themselves to draw you in? Consider thanking them in person, over the phone, by text, or with a handwritten note in the mail.

- *Take stock of your own spiritual status.* Have you surrendered to the Lord and received new life in Jesus, and so experienced the promise of Ezekiel 36:26-27? If God has turned your heart of stone to flesh and the Spirit now lives in you, take a minute to praise and worship him.

- *Pray for God to help you.* As Christ-followers we are not left to our own strength and devices. The Holy Spirit lives in us. Pause now and pray, asking God to help you grow in your desire and ability to warmly welcome others into your life and, if believers, into your faith family.

2. THE RADICAL WELCOME OF THE EARLY CHURCH

Have you ever considered how crazy it is that you worship someone who started out in this world as a humble baby placed in a manger in Bethlehem over 2,000 years ago? How wild that one man, who grew up as the son of a carpenter, garnered a following and established a faith that is now the largest in the world.[1] More than one third of all people on the planet profess to worship Jesus.[2] That's 2.3 billion of us. And to think, I am now sitting at my desk 6,873 miles away from where Jesus Christ was crucified and rose again. Yet, he is my Lord and my Savior.

From Jerusalem to Judea and Samaria, and to the ends of the earth, the name of Jesus is being proclaimed, just as he said it would be (Acts 1:8). After Jesus ascended to heaven, his followers gathered in an upper room to pray. The Bible tells us there were about 120 people there (Acts

---

1 https://www.pewresearch.org/fact-tank/2017/04/05/christians-remain-worlds-largest-religious-group-but-they-are-declining-in-europe/ (accessed Feb. 12, 2022).

2 https://www.pewresearch.org/fact-tank/2017/04/05/christians-remain-worlds-largest-religious-group-but-they-are-declining-in-europe/ (accessed Feb. 12, 2022).

1:15). Not long after that, Peter proclaimed the gospel on the day of Pentecost and "those who accepted his message were baptized, and about three thousand were added to their number that day" (Acts 2:41). And again, "the apostles were teaching the people, proclaiming in Jesus the resurrection of the dead ... many who heard the message believed; so the number of men who believed grew to about five thousand" (Acts 4:2, 4).

From 120 to 3,000 to 5,000 and on. The book of Acts is replete with stories of the proclamation of the gospel and the resulting faith of both Jews and Gentiles. Historians and sociologists say that Christianity grew at a rate of 40% per decade.[3] In Acts 1 there were about 120 Christians. Today, 2,000 years later, we number in the billions.

GROWING BY WELCOMING

As missionaries and church-planters, our family has always loved reading about the remarkable growth of the early church. The book of Acts inspires and spurs us to ask God to move like that again, wherever he's called us. The fellowship of the believers described in Acts 2:42-47 is a particular favorite. I imagine Christ-followers have marveled over this portion of Scripture for the last two millennia:

They devoted themselves to the apostles' teaching and

---

3 Rodney Stark, *The Rise of Christianity: How the Obscure, Marginal Jesus Movement Became the Dominant Religious Force in the Western World in a Few Centuries* (Harper Collins, 1996), p 7.

to fellowship, to the breaking of bread and to prayer. Everyone was filled with awe at the many wonders and signs performed by the apostles. All the believers were together and had everything in common. They sold property and possessions to give to anyone who had need. Every day they continued to meet together in the temple courts. They broke bread in their homes and ate together with glad and sincere hearts, praising God and enjoying the favor of all the people. And the Lord added to their number daily those who were being saved.

Can you imagine a warmer or more welcoming scenario? We read this account with awe and a hint of "holy jealousy". *Lord, do it again, right here, right now, we pray.*

The early church has so much to show us and teach us in the way it welcomed others in. In the chapter ahead, we will ponder not only how Christianity became the largest religion in the world but also the world's most diverse religion. No other faith exemplifies such strong unity across such great diversity. The radical welcome of the early church laid the foundation for people of all ethnicities and socioeconomic classes, as well as both sexes, to feel at home with one another in our faith family.

THE RADICAL WELCOME OF ALL ETHNICITIES
The missions agency that my husband and I serve with has mobilization bases in Canada, the United States, Ghana, Singapore, the United Kingdom, Australia, New Zealand, the Netherlands, Brazil, Egypt, South Korea, the

Dominican Republic, and the Philippines. Missionaries come from all corners of the globe to proclaim Christ all over the globe. Our gatherings are not guaranteed to be in English, and we often rise early or stay up late to meet online with colleagues in the other hemisphere.

The work of missions is not America-centric or Euro-centric because the gospel isn't either. In fact, many missionaries now hail from the Global South, as a gospel presence increases there and decreases in the north. For example, currently over 60 percent of the population in Sub-Saharan Africa profess to be Christian,[4] and by 2050, that region will likely be home to 40 percent of the professing Christian population worldwide.[5]

God's story in the Bible opens and closes with his heart for every nation and tribe. In the beginning we see his promise to Abraham that "all peoples on earth will be blessed through [him]" (Genesis 12:3). And at the end we see John's vision of heaven, including "a great multitude that no one could count, from every nation, tribe, people and language, standing before the throne and before the Lamb" (Revelation 7:9).

In the middle of the Bible, we see Jesus' Great Commission to the very first Christians, and to you and me, to "go and make disciples of all nations, baptizing them in the

---

4 https://www.pewforum.org/2015/04/02/sub-saharan-africa/ (accessed Feb. 12, 2022).

5 https://www.pewforum.org/2015/04/02/religious-projections-2010-2050/ (accessed Feb. 12, 2022).

name of the Father and of the Son and of the Holy Spirit" (Matthew 28:19). And we see that begin to happen right away in the book of Acts when Samaritans are baptized (8:12), an Ethiopian is baptized (8:38), the church in Judea, Galilee, and Samaria increases in numbers (9:31), many believe in Joppa (9:42), a great number are added to the Lord in Antioch (11:21), and many come to faith in Iconium (14:1), Derbe (14:21), Lystra (16:5), Philippi (16:15, 33), Thessalonica (17:4), Berea (17:12), Athens (17:34), Corinth (18:8), and Ephesus (19:5).

God's plan all along has been to welcome all ethnicities, nations, and tribes into his kingdom. Their presence among his people brings him glory and, in the church, the unity we see amid the diversity causes us to worship. Jesus is the peace among so many different groups—he destroys the dividing walls of hostility and reconciles us to God and to one another (Ephesians 2:14-16).

THE RADICAL WELCOME OF ALL CLASSES

God's people are also called to invite people from all classes to faith in Christ. The church which married my husband and me and sent us off to the mission field is, by God's grace, a picture of outreach to socioeconomic diversity. The church provides a free food market, addiction recovery, free legal aid, English classes, job training, and more. In these programs throughout the week and in the pews on Sunday, Christians who give and receive these services worship together and commune together. Side by side are the lawyer and the undocumented immigrant, the white-collar addict and the teen mom looking for a job, the former gang-member and the elderly man whose joy is teaching a weekly class on budgeting. They come from across the spectrum of socioeconomic backgrounds, and they are family.

The early church excelled at loving others across socioeconomic lines. The first Christians took seriously the admonishments of James, Jesus' brother and a church leader in Jerusalem. James taught the church that pure and faultless religion is to look after widows and orphans in their distress (James 1:27). He also said, "Has not God chosen those who are poor in the eyes of the world to be rich in faith and to inherit the kingdom he promised those who love him? ... If you show favoritism, you sin" (James 2:5, 9).

Documents from the first centuries reveal that early Christians obeyed these commands so obviously and joyfully that serving the disenfranchised, the poor, and the sick became a major driver of church growth. The poor and the pagans were drawn to faith in Christ by the selflessness of the first Christ-followers.

In the 4th century, the Roman emperor Julian sought to compel the pagans to be as generous as the Christians. He complained in a letter to the pagan high priest of Galatia in 362 that the generosity of the Christians was causing too much church growth and adversely affecting the pagan practices in his domain. He wrote, "I think that when the poor happened to be neglected and overlooked by the [pagan] priests, the impious Galileans [Christians] observed this and devoted themselves to benevolence ... The impious Galileans support not only their poor, but ours as well, so everyone can see that our people lack aid from us."[6]

Dionysius, a Christian bishop of Alexandria in the 3rd century, noted in one of his letters that an epidemic "terrified the pagans, [but] Christians greeted the epidemic as merely 'schooling and testing.'"[7] Further he said, "Heedless of danger, [the Christians] took charge of the sick, attending to their every need and ministering to them in Christ."[8] The earliest followers of Jesus did as their Lord did: they laid down their lives to care for those who could not pay them back.

THE RADICAL WELCOME OF WOMEN AND GIRLS

On any given Sunday, at any given Christian worship service around the world, you are likely to see more women than men. That's because Christianity is predominately female. Across the world, women are 7% more likely to attend Christian worship services than men. [9] But this is not a new phenomenon—Christianity has had a majority of female followers since the time of

6 Rodney Stark, *The Rise of Christianity*, p 83-84.

7 As above, p 82.

8 As above, p 82.

9 https://www.pewforum.org/2016/03/22/the-gender-gap-in-religion-around-the-world/ (accessed Feb. 12, 2022).

Jesus.[10] In the Greco-Roman world, Christian women enjoyed a higher status and better treatment within their Christian relationships than their pagan counterparts did within their pagan ones.

Both the Old Testament and the New Testament present clearly and boldly the value of women. Our creation story itself shows that God made both male and female *imago dei*—to reflect his image. Adam alone could not fully image God; a "helper" was necessary too. And lest you or I think that a helper is somehow inferior, the same Hebrew word is found throughout the Old Testament, most often as a description of God himself.[11] Women have been considered intrinsically "very good" since the creation of Eve.

God's valuing of and care for women is obvious throughout the New Testament too. We see the admirable characters of Mary, Elizabeth, and Anna in the very first pages of the Gospels. We see Jesus' striking forgiveness and commendation of the sinful woman who comes to lavish worship on him at the Pharisee's home (Luke 7:36-50). We see that Jesus traveled with women, and his ministry was supported by them (Luke 8:1-3). And we catch a glimpse of the ongoing and vital gospel work of many women when Paul greets Phoebe, Priscilla, Mary, Junia, Tryphena and Tryphosa, Persis, and Julia, among other unnamed women, in Romans 16.

---

10 Rodney Stark, *The Rise of Christianity,* p 128.

11 A few examples include Deuteronomy 33:29; Psalm 33:20; 70:5; 115:9-11; 121:1-2.

This welcome of women in the early church stood in stark contrast to the Greco-Roman world of the first few centuries. From the earliest moments of a girl's life, the church sought to protect her. Everything from rescuing abandoned baby girls from trash heaps (female infanticide was a common Roman practice, as families favored male offspring) to allowing their girls to marry at a later age and have a say in choosing their husbands, to protecting women from divorce, incest, infidelity, polygamy, mistreatment by their husbands, and the poverty of widowhood—all this made the first Christian communities a place of refuge and care for all women and girls.

THE CHURCH: A PORCH LIGHT IN A DARK NIGHT

2,000 years later, in the increasingly post-Christian West, it's tempting to wonder if secular voices are right when they claim that Christian churches are passé, on the wrong side of history, or even downright damaging. But here's what is true: the ailments of our age are not unlike those of the first centuries. And the power of today's church is not unlike the power of the early church. We offer the world the healing words and power of Jesus Christ. We know who it is that made us and died to save us. We are a porch light in a dark night. Like the first Christians, we offer open arms, warmth, welcome, Christ's message of hope, and bright light in a dark time.

Sociologist Rodney Stark offers compelling stories and data on the radical welcome of the early church in *The Rise of Christianity*:

To cities filled with the homeless and impoverished, Christianity offered charity as well as hope. To cities filled with newcomers and strangers, Christianity offered an immediate basis for attachments. To cities filled with orphans and widows, Christianity provided a new and expanded sense of family. To cities torn by violent ethnic strife, Christianity offered a new basis for social solidarity. And to cities faced with epidemics, fires, and earthquakes, Christianity offered effective nursing services.[12]

The early church was a city on a hill (Matthew 5:14)—a light, a beacon, a welcome to all who needed comfort and care. Christian, if we are willing, this can be said of us too. Our lives and homes can be obvious beacons of safety in dangerous places. Compelled by the Spirit, we too can stand ready to offer gospel hope and healing to all who are hurting, whatever their background.

We do well to ask ourselves: Is my church known for sacrificing itself for the good of others, for going toward the hurting and the lost, and for displaying supernatural unity in the midst of great diversity? Are we known more for our attractive facades, or for the sacrificial love and care we provide on the inside? And on an individual level: Who are the newcomers I am more likely to move towards on a Sunday—those who are just like me or those with whom I seemingly have little in common? Do

---

12 Rodney Stark, *The Rise of Christianity*, p 161.

I make space in my life, and in my schedule, for those whose lives are messy or awkward or just very different from my own? Am I more interested in cultivating comfortable friendships or in enjoying the richness that comes from embracing relationships with people from all walks of life?

Our earliest ancestors in the faith show us what a Christ-honoring welcome looks like. The believers in Acts 2 were an exceedingly diverse bunch. We marvel at how deeply committed they were to one another—breaking bread, growing in the apostles' teaching, and sharing everything with one another as anyone had need (Acts 2:42-47)—but I think we often overlook that this deep intimacy was amid great diversity. This description of the early church follows the day of Pentecost, when through the Holy Spirit, the apostles spoke to a diverse multitude of people in their own tongues. The Bible says that Parthians, Medes, Elamites, residents of Mesopotamia, Judea, Cappadocia, Pontus and Asia, Phrygia and Pamphylia, Egypt and the parts of Libya near Cyrene, visitors from Rome, Cretans and Arabs all exclaimed, "We hear ... the wonders of God in our own tongues!" (Acts 2:9-11).

Are we known today for this same depth of unity amid diversity? Our context is not unlike that of the first few centuries. As then, we bear witness to great violence, fear, division, and despair in our communities. As then, the biblical worldview is mocked and rejected as irrelevant and foolish. As then, men and women and boys and girls are harmed at the hands of those who follow secular and pagan practices. As then, there is great disparity and injustice between ethnicities, classes, and the sexes.

And as then, Jesus says, "I am the light of the world. Whoever follows me will never walk in darkness, but will have the light of life" (John 8:12). May you and I shine brightly. May we be a city on a hill. May we "let [our] light shine before others, that they may see [our] good deeds and glorify [our] Father in heaven" (Matthew 5:16). Do it again Lord, we pray.

ACTION STEPS

The radical welcome of the early church can feel so overwhelming that it can be paralyzing. As we glimpse their incredible ministry, we might be tempted to compare ourselves and fall short in despair. Let's acknowledge that we are finite humans and that God has appointed a specific time and place for us to live in. With that foundation, let's consider the particular ways each one of us might pursue the welcome of others in the context where God has placed us.

- *Ponder the past growth and current size of the Christian family across the globe.* Look around Operation World's website (https://operationworld.org). Pray for the country they have highlighted for today and consider signing up to pray for the "Operation World Country of the Day" every day.

- *Visit the census website for your country, where you can investigate demographic data for your local community.* Check out the maps on the site and find out what the ethnic and socioeconomic makeup of your community is. Does any of the information surprise you? Is your church meeting some of the needs you see reflected on these maps, or do you know of a local ministry that is? Consider whether you should get involved.

- *Reflect on the role and value of women in your church family.* Consider asking a woman in a ministry role in your church if you could talk to her sometime about this issue. Do women inside your church feel valued, protected, and equipped to serve? Are there ways in which your church is ministering to marginalized women outside your church?

- *Search your own heart for any hint of ethnocentrism or racism, classism, sexism, or any other ungodly way in which you may subconsciously view people who are not like you.* Consider inviting a godly and trusted friend to join you in this self-reflection. Are there books or podcasts or other resources that you could take advantage of to better understand the plight of those on the margins of your community?

- *Speak to someone different this Sunday.* Make a beeline for the person who seems furthest away from you in worldly terms, smile, and say hello! You'll likely find much common ground as you chat.

- *Pray for gospel unity in your local church, as well as gospel unity across the global Christian family.* Discord, dissensions, and factions are works of the flesh (Galatians 5:19-20), while the fruit of the Spirit is love, joy, peace, forbearance, kindness, goodness, faithfulness, gentleness and self-control (v 22-23). Pray that you and brothers and sisters in Christ in your church would deny the flesh and grow in the Spirit.

3. THIS CHURCH OPENS WIDE HER DOORS

Every Sunday, our worship service opens with a Welcome Liturgy: a set of words which begins the service and sets the tone for the whole morning. While the liturgies used in other parts of the service change each week, the words of welcome always stay the same:

> To all who are weary, and need rest; to all who mourn, and long for comfort; to all who fail, and desire strength; to all who sin, and need a Savior, this church opens wide her doors with a welcome from Jesus himself, the Friend of sinners.[13]

These words of welcome have been popularized over the last several years by Ray Ortlund, the founding pastor of Immanuel Nashville, where the Welcome originated and is still repeated week in and week out. Like my own church, many others have followed Immanuel Nashville's lead.

---

13 https://immanuelnashville.com/sundays (accessed Jul. 14, 2022).

The weekly repetition of this Welcome does two important things for both visitors and church members. First, it says to the visitor that *all* are welcome here. It tells each attendee that it's ok to not be ok. It tells every visitor that no one in this church is perfect. No one has arrived. We are all weary. We all fail. We all need the welcome of Jesus, the Friend of sinners. The liturgy says, *We know you have issues, and we do too.*

Second, and probably more powerfully, the liturgy weekly renews the minds of the church members. Those who arrive weary and heavy-laden are reminded that that's ok. They are reminded that God's love and grace is sufficient for them—they aren't too much for God or his church. And, at the other end of the spectrum, for those who arrive with pride and a sense that they have it all together, the liturgy serves as a gentle rebuke. The words are a reproof and a reminder that no one has arrived—no, not one. The liturgy says, *If you need a Savior—and that's all of us—then, welcome. He, and we, welcome you in.*

OUTSIDERS LOOKING IN

Data show that this message bears repeating. While we who attend church regularly most likely feel at home there, our positive perspective is not shared by those on the outside. Recent surveys conducted by the Barna Group reveal a huge gap between how churchgoers view the church and how nonattenders feel about it.

According to Barna, 80% of practicing Christians have a positive view of the church, while only 21% of non-Christians think of the church in a positive way. Half of non-Christians don't trust the pastors in their local community, while 85% of Christians do. And over half of those aged 22-36 think the local church is detached from the real issues people are facing.[14]

The Welcome Liturgy is one way to begin to address these discouraging statistics. It's a weekly renewal that transforms the way we think about God, ourselves, and each other. The Welcome fosters in us humility, compassion, and regular repentance. It removes our guard, dismantles arrogance, and allows us to embrace the truth that we are all works in progress. From the senior pastor through the most recent visitor, we are all sinners in need of a Savior.

But the Welcome Liturgy is only the start. So how can our churches (whatever their liturgical style or absence of one) foster a spirit of authenticity among us—such that, with God's help, the perception of the church held by those on the outside is softened and improved, one humble relationship at a time?

---

14 All statistics in this paragraph are from Carey Nieuwhof, "The Self-Awareness Gap: What Non-Christian People Really Think about the Church"; https://careynieuwhof.com/the-self-awareness-gap-what-non-christian-people-really-think-about-the-church/ (accessed Mar. 10, 2022).

THE CHURCH IS A HOSPITAL

It starts with having a clear view of what church is. It has been said, "The church is a hospital for sinners, not a museum for saints."[15] It's a striking word picture as it calls to mind images of people who are unwell but want to get better—people who acknowledge their sickness, are humbled by it, and have placed themselves in the hands of others who might help them.

Closely related to the word "hospital", is the word "hospitality". The root of both is the Latin noun *hospes*, meaning "one who provides lodging or entertainment for a guest or visitor."[16] Hospitals provide hospitality to the sick so that they might become healthy and whole.

And that is exactly what God calls us to do. Both the Old and New Testaments command those who belong to the Lord to generously provide hospitality. And not only are we to practice hospitality, but we are to do so in a way that—if necessary—administers aid and care to the sick. The prophet Isaiah says true fasting is "to share your food with the hungry and to provide the poor wanderer with shelter" (Isaiah 58:7). Paul tells Titus that an elder must be hospitable (Titus 1:8). While in the home of a prominent Pharisee, Jesus commands, "When you give a banquet, invite the poor, the crippled, the lame, the

---

15 I believe this quote originates with Abigail Van Buren in a Dear Abby syndicated column, January 29, 2001; https://www.sun-sentinel.com/news/fl-xpm-2000-01-29-0001280652-story.html (accessed Mar. 10, 2022).

16 https://www.merriam-webster.com/words-at-play/word-history-hospital-hostel-hotel-hospice (accessed Mar. 10, 2022).

blind, and you will be blessed. Although they cannot repay you, you will be repaid at the resurrection of the righteous" (Luke 14:13-14). And the apostle Peter urges the church to "offer hospitality to one another without grumbling" (1 Peter 4:9).

Over and over the Bible commands the church to open wide our doors to the hungry, the poor, the wanderer, the crippled, the lame, the blind, and to one another. What we might easily dismiss or forget, though, is that *we, the church*, are the hungry, the poor, the wanderer, the crippled, the lame, and the blind:

> *When the teachers of the law who were Pharisees saw [Jesus] eating with the sinners and tax collectors, they asked his disciples: "Why does he eat with tax collectors and sinners?" On hearing this, Jesus said to them, "It is not the healthy who need a doctor, but the sick. I have not come to call the righteous, but sinners."*
>
> *(Mark 2:16-17)*

We who gather in church are the sick in need of a doctor. We are the sinners in need of a Savior. To be sure, by God's immeasurable love and grace, we who are in Christ are redeemed. We are now new creations, and God lives inside of us, but we have not yet reached perfection. We still wage war against our own flesh. We will not be without sin until we reach heaven. We are still in need of, even as we are required to give, the hospitality of a hospital. And praise God—that is exactly what Jesus' mission provides for us.

THE MISSION OF JESUS

In our wealthy Western context, it can be easy to lose sight of the reality that Jesus came for the sick and the poor, the oppressed and the hurting. Even in the church we can drift toward self-sufficiency and fool ourselves into thinking that we're just fine. But Jesus' mission was one of rescue and healing—and it's one that you and I and the whole world need, no matter how materially comfortable we are.

The Gospel of Luke tells how Jesus began his public ministry by preaching in the synagogue in his hometown of Nazareth. One Sabbath, he read from the scroll of the prophet Isaiah, written hundreds of years before, saying:

The Spirit of the Lord is on me,
because he has anointed me
to proclaim good news to the poor.
He has sent me to proclaim freedom for the prisoners
and recovery of sight for the blind,
to set the oppressed free,
to proclaim the year of the Lord's favor. (Luke 4:18-19)

Jesus rolled up the scroll and, with the eyes of everyone in the synagogue fastened on him, declared, "Today this scripture is fulfilled in your hearing" (Luke 4:21).

Jesus was proclaiming to the synagogue worshipers that he was God and that his mission was to bring good news, to bring freedom, and to bring healing. The gospel is good news! The gifts of our God are very good.

So then, when we gather to worship our God, we too should be marked by this kind of goodness.

And yet the stereotype of the church is that we are grumpy. Or snobby. Perhaps a crowd of curmudgeons. Or a country club with weekly meetings. We are not always or even often associated with proclaiming good news to the poor, or drawing near to prisoners to set them free, or befriending the blind to bring them sight.

While it's only a stereotype, we should be honest in admitting that stereotypes do originate somewhere. So think for a moment about the conversations you've had with other believers this past week. Or consider your immediate thoughts when an outsider came into your church. To what extent did they reflect the gracious invitation of our Savior? Let's be honest about some of our ugly tendencies and reflexes, and ask the Lord to help us joyfully make space for everyone he draws near to.

When Jesus said, "The Spirit of the Lord is on me," he was pronouncing that he was the anointed one of God. He understood his mission as the promised Messiah. He was pronouncing to his community that God had come down, as he said he would, and that he had come to save the lost and heal the sick. This is who our God is. And Jesus says to us Christians, "Follow me." This mission, then, of good news and freedom and healing, is ours too.

WELCOMED IN BY GOD'S PEOPLE

There's a family in our church who does an exceptional job of reaching out and offering hospitality to their neighbors. The wife walks the neighborhood most mornings and prays for each household, paper in hand with the names and needs of the people who live inside each home. Along with her husband and young children, she hosts block parties; they have each household over for dinner one at a time. We were delighted to see several of their nonbelieving neighbors at our Christmas Eve service.

Just this past weekend, as I was preparing to write this very chapter, my friend called to tell me that one of their neighbors had accepted their invitation to the small group that they host through our church. The neighbor, a man who is not yet a follower of Jesus, was reeling because his wife had just left him and their teen children. In his shock and heartache, he knew where to turn. He knew where he would be warmly received, embraced, and cared for—at the home of the Christians on his street.

He sat in on their small group and received the nourishment of good food and kind new friends. They all opened their Bibles together, and he had the chance to read the good news with his own eyes. He told the group that he'd never read the Bible for himself, and that that night it was starting to come alive to him. I saw him in our worship service just this morning. He heard and read our Welcome Liturgy. He was fed by the worship and the word. He was warmly embraced by God's people.

He received hospitality in our hospital. God is at work in this midst of his pain.

Our friends, their small group, and now our whole church have had the opportunity to proclaim freedom, healing, and salvation to this man. Because of the humble kindness of our friends to their neighbors, he knew where to turn for help. He did not perceive in them pride or "perfection", or an air of "get it together"; he was not met with a closed-off clique in their small group. He saw in them Jesus, Friend of sinners.

If you're like me, this family's example spurs you to consider how your neighbors see you. Do the people in your neighborhood or workplace see you as someone who would offer them care and kindness during a crisis? How might you begin to build such a reputation in your setting?

COMMUNION AND COMMUNITY

But—praise God—we don't do this alone. Showing hospitality is a whole-church-family endeavor. And, if you have eyes to see it, there are likely many people in your church who are extending this kind of welcome to the broken and needy.

One of my favorite parts of our service is when we participate in of the Lord's Supper after the sermon each week. After I collect my bread and wine, I stand with my husband at the back of the sanctuary to join him in praying for anyone who requests prayer. As we wait for people to come to us, I scan the crowd, and my heart swells. I silently praise the Lord for all he has done in and through our congregation.

I see families who are fostering children in need—but they don't stop there. They come alongside these little ones' moms and dads and do all they can to help them come clean from drugs, get stable housing, and be ready to be reunited with their children. I see medical-school students who spend their free time offering free medical care in homeless shelters. I see brothers and sisters who are honest about their abuse of drugs and alcohol, and I see those who are walking alongside them, ensuring they get the professional and relational help that each one needs. I see couples who are honest about the dire state of their marriages and the friends who are helping them to mend what's broken. I see young couples who have lost babies and their friends who do not hesitate to lament alongside them. I see weariness, but I also see real rest that comes from our God, the comfort of his Spirit, and the embrace of his people.

And I know the same is happening in churches all over the world. My friend with a teen child who wants to transition genders has been warmly embraced by her church in another part of the state. My friend with a son who has severe disabilities is welcomed into worship every Sunday in another state. Her church family knows that her son will be loud and disruptive, but they don't mind. Friends in Europe house refugees in their church, turning pews into beds and fellowship halls into cafeterias. Friends in Asia must welcome others in secret—which they do, and at great risk. They invite the outcast, the widow, and those formerly imprisoned into their family of Christ, which meets underground.

Christians on every continent know that as we have been welcomed, so we must also welcome others. It's humbling, beautiful, and the work of our kind and hospitable God. As you consider your own life, neighborhood, and calling, where might you begin to welcome others in? How can you make space for the sick and the poor, the oppressed and the hurting?

CHRIST'S LOVE COMPELS US

In Paul's second letter to the Corinthians, he says, "Christ's love compels us ... he died for all, that those who live should no longer live for themselves but for him who died for them" (2 Corinthians 5:14-15). Paul was compelled by Christ's love to live for God's glory and for the good of others. In seeking the good of others, he pursued their reconciliation with the God who made them and died to save them.

Today, we share in the same task. There's a sense in which, along with Paul, we, the church, are now Christ's ambassadors, "as though God were making his appeal through us. We implore [others] on Christ's behalf: Be reconciled to God" (2 Corinthians 5:20).

Ambassadors are sent as representatives of the sovereign who sent them. As Christians, we represent our God:

"While we were God's enemies, we were reconciled to him through the death of his Son" (Romans 5:10). And our role now is to represent God's immeasurable mercy and compassion to those who are yet his enemies and, by the power of God's Spirit, to reconcile these lost ones to our good God.

It's true that the recent Barna surveys of those outside the church paint a discouraging picture. Churches are not largely seen in a positive light and we churchgoers are too often better known for our judgment, condemnation, and seclusion than we are for our welcome. But faithful Christians, who are compelled by Christ's love, know *they themselves* are weary and need rest, and that *they themselves* sin and need a Savior.

May we be welcoming Christians who walk in the welcome of Jesus and extend it to others. May we create welcoming churches that long to reconcile others to Jesus. May we open wide our doors and make space for everyone.

ACTION STEPS

What a generous and undeserved welcome you and I have received from Christ and his church. And what a relief it is to be welcomed on the merits of Christ and not our own! As we remember how we were welcomed in, let's consider how we might open wide the doors of our church meetings, homes, and hearts to welcome others in.

- *Ask some of your nonbelieving friends and family what they think of Christian churches in your community.* Find out if their perspectives are positive or negative and seek to understand their reasons. Receive their critiques in good faith, as an opportunity to grow. The conversation may provide a chance to apologize for the sins of the church and to share the desire with your loved ones that you hope to do better on behalf of the church.

■ *Take a minute to reflect on what it's like to enter a new church—maybe from your first time visiting your current church or when you visited another church.* What contributed to your impression that the people were welcoming (or not)? Did you get a sense that they were aware that they too were sinners in need of a Savior?

■ *Reflect on whether your church portrays a spirit of opening wide her doors.* Put yourself in the shoes of a visitor. What things are present that tell them your congregation is weary, mourns, fails, and sins? What might be missing?

■ *Ponder whether you count yourself among the sick and the sinners that Jesus came for.* Do you see yourself in his words in Mark 2:17: "It is not the healthy who need a doctor, but the sick. I have not come to call the righteous, but sinners"?

■ *Pray and ask the Lord to show you how you might personally practice the ministry of reconciliation in your own neighborhood, workplace, or community.* Ask God to show you who needs to hear his message of redemption. Write down the names of those people and pray for them. Ask the Lord to give you boldness, as Christ's love compels you, to implore others on Jesus' behalf.

4. WELCOME TO
THE FAMILY

Last fall I spoke at a conference for women who are missionaries all over the world. The women came from many different nations and had spent years and lifetimes proclaiming Christ in many different contexts. Just before the third session in which I was supposed to teach, the time of worship included a song about the universal church. The lyrics spoke to the birth of the church after Jesus' resurrection, and to the diversity and spread of the church across the globe over the last 2,000 years.

As I looked around the room at the various skin tones and clothing styles, and recalled stories the women had shared with me over the last couple of days, I was overcome with emotion. It's not the best look for a public speaker, but I could not control my tears. These women, who I had not known just days prior, were my sisters. I reflected on my own family of origin with heartache and longing, as most of my relatives still reject Christ. But here I was, singing the praises of Jesus, our older brother (Hebrews 2:11), with my sisters. This was my family.

I arrived on stage with tears still streaming, and it took me a minute to recover. Many in the audience were also crying. Missions can be lonely. But we were relishing our family reunion and praising our Father in heaven together. We belonged to God, and we belonged to each other.

A HUNDRED TIMES AS MANY MOTHERS, SISTERS, AND BROTHERS

So far, we've considered Jesus' welcome of us (chapter 1), the example of the early church in their embrace of people from all backgrounds (chapter 2), and how we might begin to create an atmosphere in our own churches which expresses Jesus' own heart for the sinners and sufferers who come through our doors for the first time (chapter 3).

But that's only the beginning. Once people become Christians—or when those who are already believers move into the area and join our fellowship—they don't remain guests or newcomers forever; they're meant to become part of our family.

I know firsthand how important this is. When my husband and I left for the mission field with our six-month-old firstborn child, our parents were understandably distressed. She was the first grandchild on both sides, and we were setting out for a lifetime on the other side of the world. With travel between Okinawa and Colorado requiring at least three flights, about 30 hours, and a considerable amount of money, we knew we wouldn't see our family often. Well-meaning friends and family worried: "How will you raise your children without their grandparents, aunts, and uncles nearby?" We were young, naïve, and hopeful, but we didn't have a well-thought-out answer.

There were moments when, on the opposite side of the planet from our parents and siblings, I felt like the disciple Peter, who said to Jesus, "We have left everything to follow you" (Mark 10:28). I may not have outwardly spoken as brazenly as Peter, but I could inwardly hear my heart in his words.

Jesus' response held me fast then, and it holds me fast now. He said to Peter and all the disciples, "Truly I tell you ... no one who has left home or brothers or sisters or mother or father or children or fields for me and the gospel will fail to receive a hundred times as much in this present age: homes, brothers, sisters, mothers, children and fields—along with persecutions—and in the age to come eternal life" (Mark 10:29-30).

Jesus says that if you must forsake your family to follow him, you will receive a hundred times more in this age and in the age to come eternal life. Persecutions will also be present, he warns, but they will be met with abundant blessings. Our family in Christ will *more than* make up for any family lost when we pursue Jesus and the gospel.

What a relief to know that our God provides. And what a responsibility too: just as Jesus promises to provide a family for us, so too he uses *us* to provide a family for others. So how do we become that kind of church?

HERE ARE MY MOTHERS AND BROTHERS

It starts with taking Jesus' words seriously. At one point during his public ministry, Jesus was talking to a crowd when his mother and brothers showed up, wanting to speak with him. In response Jesus said, "'Who is my mother, and who are my brothers?' Pointing to his disciples, he said, 'Here are my mother and my brothers. For whoever does the will of my Father in heaven is my brother and sister and mother'" (Matthew 12:48-50).

Jesus gives us a new definition of "family". Whoever does the will of God the Father is in his family. The temporary families that we are born into and marry into are superseded by the eternal family we have in Christ. As Christians, our family in Christ is meant to take priority over our earthly family. Of course, the Scriptures are clear that we are to love and care for our own households (1 Timothy 5:8). We must not neglect our earthly families. But I suspect that most of us are more likely to neglect our spiritual families. How often do we place our spiritual families in their rightful place? Do we make plenty of space for our spiritual siblings alongside our biological ones?

To our individualistic and Western ears, this is a hard truth to hear. For one thing, we love our autonomy. We identify as unique individuals first and foremost. We do not want to be beholden to others. The reflex of our flesh and the instinct of our culture is to make choices and spend our time in the way that's best for us. Even when we do speak about "family" inside the church, it's almost exclusively about the nuclear family. Just consider how many Christian ministries are dedicated to families, marriages, parenthood, and raising children. And please hear me: these ministries are edifying and necessary. But I do think we have a blind spot when it comes to focusing on our natural families to the neglect of our spiritual family.

Putting together what Jesus said to Peter and what he said when his mother and brothers wanted to speak to him, we see that our spiritual family is primary and eternal, and our physical families are secondary and temporary. When Jesus rescues us and makes us one of his own, we get a whole new identity and family in him.

Our new family is both global and local. When I was overcome with emotion at that missions conference, it was because of my gratitude to the Lord for the multitude of godly sisters he had given me around the whole world. While I sometimes grieve the lack of faith in my own family of origin, I rejoice in the depth and breadth of faith in my global spiritual family.

But while those missionaries are indeed my sisters, they are not my local faith family. The universal church is like our extended family—the sum of the millions of local churches all over the globe. The local church is our "immediate" faith family, where we are meant to grow our roots, so that we thrive and flourish in our faith. The assumption of the entire New Testament is that as you and I surrender to Jesus and join the big church, we will give our lives over to life in a local church. While wildly countercultural and counter to our flesh, surrendering our lives to Jesus and a local faith family is God's will, it's for our good, and it's for the good of others.

BEYOND A CASUAL WELCOME

Church membership and attendance are both down across the Western world (even as both are on the rise in the Global South, which is worth rejoicing over!). A quarter of a century ago, 70% of Americans belonged to a church, a synagogue, or a mosque. In 2020, only 47% did so.[17] Of all who claim to be Christians in the US, just 44% attend church services at least weekly or more.[18]

When my family lived in Europe, we noted that the vast majority of churches stood empty—hollow museums to a faith that once existed among the people but no more. Across the continent only 2.9% of Europeans claim to be evangelical Christians.[19]

---

17 https://news.gallup.com/poll/341963/church-membership-falls-below-majority-first-time.aspx (accessed Mar. 13, 2022).

18 https://www.pewforum.org/2019/10/17/in-u-s-decline-of-christianity-continues-at-rapid-pace/ (accessed Mar. 13, 2022).

19 https://www.joshuaproject.net/continents/EUR (accessed Mar. 13, 2022).

Where I live now, in Colorado, church attendance and membership are especially low compared to the rest of the nation. People move to our state to enjoy outdoor recreation on the weekends, not to go to church. Even when Christians who were once church members in another state relocate here, local pastors say it feels like an uphill battle to convince attendees that weekly attendance and even membership are for their good.

The thing about familial relationships is they're not meant to be carried out in casual, occasional get-togethers. Families are meant to have intimacy, and frequent and deep interaction. Relationships with mothers, brothers, fathers, and sisters cannot be maintained by a quick hello in the fellowship hall a couple times a month. Our membership in the global faith family of Jesus is meant to be seen in our abiding participation in a local faith family.

THRIVING IN YOUR LOCAL FAITH FAMILY

As you are reading this book, you are likely already convinced that belonging to a local faith family is important. But it is probable that even committed church members will eventually run into one of two issues.

The first issue is that we get too cozy in our years-old cliques, such that we're slow to embrace newcomers. When we find ourselves in such a group, it's good for us to be reminded and spurred to welcome others in.

The second issue is on the other end of the spectrum. Some church members despair that their churches will ever feel like family. People in this second group have been trying to connect deeply with others for a while but need encouragement to persevere in finding or creating the intimacy they long for.

An intimate family is exactly what the New Testament assumes for Christians—one where everyone is welcome and deep connections are routinely forged. While we may not see the words "church membership" in the Bible, at least three New Testament realities show us what it looks like to belong to a local church (whether or not our church has a formal category of "membership").

Locale

Throughout the New Testament specific churches are mentioned, which gathered in people's homes. There was the church that met at Aquila and Priscilla's house (1 Corinthians 16:19), the church at Nympha's house (Colossians 4:15), and the church that met in Philemon's house (Philemon 1:2). More broadly, most of the epistles in the New Testament are addressed to specific groups of Christians in specific cities. The churches in Corinth or Colossae or Ephesus or Galatia were not vague, ephemeral communities.

To be a member of a local church, then, is to commit to a local group of people. It is to belong to people with whom you regularly and deeply commune. It is to gather regularly to share meals, joys, sorrows, burdens, expenses, child-rearing, and whatever else life presents you with. Church life is daily, local, and close—both geographically and relationally.

Leaders

In the book of Hebrews, Christians are instructed to "have confidence in your leaders and submit to their authority, because they keep watch over you as those who must give an account. Do this so that their work will be a joy, not a burden, for that would be of no benefit to you" (Hebrews 13:17). Additionally, in Peter's first letter, he instructs elders to "be shepherds of God's flock that is under your care" (1 Peter 5:2). He tells younger believers to "submit yourselves to your elders" (v 5a) and directs that everyone should "clothe yourselves with humility toward one another" (v 5b).

As countercultural and counter to our flesh as this feels, church membership looks like willing and joyful submission to godly leaders in our faith families, as we gladly allow them to speak God's word into our lives.

One Another

The New Testament includes over 50 commands to Christians for how we are to treat one another. Author and church elder Tim Challies points out "They do not address a relationship to God or a relationship to oneself. Neither do they speak to a relationship with the universal church. Rather, they address interpersonal relationships within a community of believers."[20] To be a member of a local church is to treat one another in the ways listed below (and more—this is only a sample.):

- "Be devoted to one another in love. Honor one another above yourselves" (Romans 12:10).

- "Accept one another, then, just as Christ accepted you, in order to bring praise to God" (Romans 15:7).

- "Be completely humble and gentle; be patient, bearing with one another in love" (Ephesians 4:2).

- "Encourage one another daily, as long as it is called 'Today,' so that none of you may be hardened by sin's deceitfulness" (Hebrews 3:13).

- "Therefore confess your sins to each other and pray for each other so that you may be healed" (James 5:16).

Church life looks like being devoted and being patient with one another. It looks like being humble and gentle, and bearing with one another in daily life-on-life relationships. Church membership is a gift. To be sure, it requires effort and self-sacrifice, and asking the Lord to help us. It also requires patience. Relationships take time to grow (often more time than we expect). But God's

---

20 https://www.challies.com/articles/one-another-the-bible-community/ (accessed Mar. 13, 2022).

design is for our good. When we make space for everyone and commit deeply to one another, we thrive.

IT'S FOR YOUR OWN GOOD

When we lived in Japan, it was for the purpose of serving the American military personnel stationed there. Military personnel and their families stayed in our community for as little as six months, or for as long as three or four years. As we've kept in touch with our military friends over the last two decades, we've had a front-row seat on a whole group of people whose church rhythms regularly get disrupted and the effects of that.

What we've observed has been surprising. Over decades of people leaving our military church and transitioning elsewhere around the globe, those with strong faith years down the road aren't necessarily the ones who were church leaders, or attendees who showed up to every mid-week event back in Okinawa. They aren't necessarily the ones who gave super generously or those with massive Christian libraries. They aren't necessarily the attendees in Japan who scrubbed the church toilets or those who witnessed to their neighbors. While those attributes were often present in the lives of those who persevere in the faith, they are not *the* common denominator.

The common denominator we have observed in Christians who persevere is how quickly they committed to a new faith family as soon as they moved to a new location. They were strongly committed to ours when we first got to know them, and then, when they landed on distant shores, they quickly found a new local church and became strongly committed there. They dive in head first and press on in their race toward Jesus wherever the military takes them.

Christians suffer in isolation because we are not meant to be alone. We were created for community. When Adam was alone, God said it wasn't good, and he made Eve (Genesis 2:18). The wisdom of Solomon tells us that two, and even three, are better than one for our own productivity, safety, and thriving (Ecclesiastes 4:9-12). We see breathtaking beauty in the early Christians who devoted themselves to the apostles' teaching, fellowship, eating together, praying together, and having all things in common (Acts 2:42-47).

We need each other. There is no Christian hack or shortcut or way around this reality. To persevere in the faith—to press on toward Jesus—Christians need one another. So dive in head first.

IT'S FOR THEIR GOOD TOO

This isn't just for your sake. The apostle Paul often wrote about the church as a body. He says, "Just as a body, though one, has many parts, but all its many parts form one body, so it is with Christ" (1 Corinthians 12:12). He explains:

Now if the foot should say, 'Because I am not a hand, I do not belong to the body,' it would not for that reason

stop being part of the body … But in fact God has
placed the parts in the body, every one of them, just as
he wanted them to be. If they were all one part, where
would the body be? As it is, there are many parts, but
one body. (1 Corinthians 12:15-20)

When God calls us to his family, he gives each one of us a role and a function. If we do not carry these out, others suffer. Across the globe, we who are in the family of Jesus need one another. I think of our family friend Nadia, who is a Muslim-background Christian from Tanzania. She has surrendered her life to Jesus but has been vehemently rejected by her biological family. She needs her local church, and her local church needs her. Or our Czech friend Martin, who has been denied professional promotions because he claims Christ in a predominantly atheistic country. He needs the local church, and his local church needs him. Or my own young adult daughters, who come from a legacy of faith but live far away from home. They need their local churches, and their local churches need them.

Brothers and sisters, we are not our own; we were bought at a price (1 Corinthians 6:19-20). We belong to God, and we belong to each other. Let us honor him and love one another well, by giving ourselves fully to our local faith families as we in turn invite others in.

ACTION STEPS

Committing to a local church is both counter to our culture and counter to our flesh, but it is for our good and for our joy! Let us consider how we might spur one another on toward the Bible's call to belong to a church family.

- *Consider both your global faith family and your local faith family.* Do you think of your brothers and sisters in Christ as your real family? Do you consider your spiritual family as eternal and primary?

- *Reflect on how the Lord has provided mothers, brothers and sisters to you in your local church.* Take some time to thank God for them. Write them a note or a text to let them know that you are thankful for God's provision to you in them.

- *If you are not yet a member of your local church, research what the process is for you to become one.* Consider reaching out to the church elders and asking them if you can meet over coffee to understand their vision for church membership.

- *Invest in new relationships.* How much time do you spend enjoying established friendships at church versus forming new ones? Are you getting the balance right? Choose a newer member to invite for dinner or coffee this week.

- *Pray for your church family and all your local siblings in Christ.* Before Jesus was betrayed and hung on the cross, he prayed to the Father and asked him to make his followers one, as the Father and Son are one (John 17:11). Pray for unity in your church body; ask the Lord to help you carry out all the "one another" commands in the Bible. Praise God for the family you have in him.

5. WELCOMING WAY
BEYOND SUNDAY

"I'm serving soup and pierogi for twelve! Among the twelve who came in last night, nine were on a train that the Russians shot at. One [of the other passengers] died and had to be carried away in a stretcher. This group is very traumatized. Please pray for the four women and eight children."

These words came from my friend and colleague Carol Lynn, who lives in Poland. She and her husband, Craig, are church planters near the Ukrainian border, and she's been sending out texts to keep a group of us updated on their efforts to help refugees fleeing the conflict. When the war broke out, our friends and their Polish church jumped right into action serving their neighbors.

On the first day when people began to flee, Craig drove their van to the border and saw hundreds—maybe thousands—of Ukrainians crossing into Poland. Droves of women and children were now outside of their war-torn land, but most didn't have an immediate place to go to. Because Craig and Carol Lynn also used to be missionaries in Russia, they can speak both Russian and Polish, making communication with most Ukrainians possible. Craig got out of his van and entered the crowd, asking who needed help.

And this began his months of almost daily trips to the border, filling his van with fleeing women and children, and bringing them back to his home, where Carol Lynn prepared food and beds for everyone. They said the groups usually stayed for a couple days, often waiting on an aunt or grandmother to join them. After a brief stay, Craig and Carol Lynn would take the sojourners to the train station, from where they would head further into Europe and further away from the war.

Carol Lynn and Craig and countless others simply did what they could with what they had. When war broke out, they didn't retreat into their own homes or weigh the pros and cons of jumping in to help. By God's grace, they simply made space for those in need. They housed well over a hundred Ukrainians in the months after the beginning of the war.

If you're like me and live thousands of miles away in a peaceful neighborhood, my friends' situation perhaps feels very far off. Nor are we all called to cross oceans and continents to proclaim Christ among people still unreached with the gospel. But here's what can be easy to forget, or perhaps feel too daunting to remember: we *are* all called to go out of our own homes and churches and comfort zones to minister to those whom God has placed near us.

A MISSIONARY MINDSET

Our first church, which I have mentioned a couple times in previous chapters, had a slogan that resonated 20 years ago and still resonates today: *Every member a missionary*. The idea is that every person who attends the church has a mission—no one is exempt.

It's tempting to view pastors and church staff as the professional Christians. They're the ones with seminary degrees and the real know-how when it comes to ministry. It's easy to think, "I can't serve my community. I don't have the answers or the skills". But, as we have already seen, the Bible doesn't give us this option. We are all called to offer light in a dark world—to be a city on a hill (Matthew 5:14-15).

If you're a Christian, you're a missionary. You may not be called to a foreign land with unreached people, but you are absolutely called to share Christ right where you are. Welcome to the mission field!

So far in the book we've mainly looked at how we can welcome those who come to *us*. But how can we *go* to those who may never approach a church or a Christian? How do we extend a welcome not just on Sundays but beyond that too—to the people around us on every other day of the week?

LOVE OF THE STRANGER

In her book *The Gospel Comes with a House Key*, Rosaria Butterfield admonishes Christians in the West to practice radically ordinary hospitality. This hospitality is radical in that it's a regular and sacrificial opening of one's home—unlike the seclusion and privacy that most people prefer. But it's ordinary in that it's not fancy or well planned or overthought. Radically ordinary hospitality pursues others, and it lays down one's own ease to welcome others in. But it is not pretentious or showy. It's using what you've got to further God's kingdom. And while that's still far from a literal warzone calling, it can still be scary.

Butterfield says, "Too many of us are sidelined by fears. We fear that people will hurt us. We fear that people will negatively influence our children. We fear that we do not even understand the language of this new world order, least of all its people ... [But] the best days are ahead. Jesus advances from the front of the line."[21]

Don't you love Butterfield's joy and optimism? She says the best days are ahead. It's true that the "post-Christian" climate we live in can be paralyzing. She's right that many of us are sidelined by fear. But, as followers of Jesus, we need not shrink back. We belong to the risen Savior, who advances from the frontlines. Our God *overcame death* to bring us life! So we can join the author of Hebrews

21 Rosaria Butterfield, *The Gospel Comes with a House Key* (Crossway, 2018), p 35.

and "say with confidence, 'The Lord is my helper; I will not be afraid. What can mere mortals do to me?'" (Hebrews 13:6)?

We belong to the eternal God, who conquered death. And he is our helper. May we be found, then, moving towards the stranger in love.

Remember, *every member a missionary*. That's you and me and everyone else in our local churches. As missionaries in our specific contexts, we all have three tasks before us. First, we must study the people in our communities. Second, we must pray. And third, we must go.

Are you ready?

KNOW YOUR PEOPLE GROUP

This first step might sound intuitive, but I fear it's often overlooked. As individuals and as whole-church families, we can easily become so consumed with our own lives and to-do lists that we forget to consider the lost people around us. As a church, we might get so bogged down with our own year-end goals or budgets or needs or parking-lot headaches, that we overlook the men and women, and boys and girls, in our own cities.

So stop for a moment and consider your community. Who are the people who live in your neighborhoods and near your church?

- Are you in a rural or urban setting, and how does that impact how you meet people?

- What are the socioeconomic factors affecting your community? Do the people around you struggle with having too little or too much, or is there a mix?

- What ethnicities are in your community? What are the histories of those ethnicities, and how do the various groups interact with one another? How might their histories impact how they interact with you or your church?

- What's your city or village like? What's the government like? Are there structures in place (schools, parks, corporations, community calendars, traditions) that help or hinder your ability to make new friendships? Is the culture in your area hostile, receptive, or apathetic toward spiritual things?

- What felt needs can you identify in your community? This may sound obvious, but felt needs are the needs that people *feel*. You may know they need the gospel, but they may not yet *feel* that. Their felt needs might be for tangible things like food, shelter, or access to education. Or their felt needs might be more relational if people in your area are isolated and lonely. Felt needs are sometimes obvious, but other times they're hard to identify until after you've developed some relationships in your sphere.

This list of questions to consider could go on for many more pages, but you get the point. Every good missionary seeks to be a student of their culture. So let's pay attention to what people outside our churches are dealing with every day. Let's ask ourselves and one another: How can we serve our neighborhood? How can we show this community that we see them, love them, and want to meet them right where they are?

WAGE WAR IN THE HEAVENLY REALMS

As Rosaria Butterfield says, we are on the frontlines. This is not a drill. As we seek to bring the gospel to people who don't yet know it, the forces of darkness will be eager to devour us (Ephesians 6:12). So while it's true we must spend time in our communities and get to know the people around us, we must also pray. In the Western world, where *doing* is usually elevated above *being*, prayer is often an afterthought or a quick way to close a meeting. But followers of Jesus know that the war for souls is waged in the heavenly realms and our most powerful weapon is prayer.

The church in South Korea is an inspiring leader when it comes to prayer. My Korean friends tell me that the Korean church gathers to pray every single morning. The majority of church members get up before the sun and gather at their church building to pray with one another before they head off to work and school. During their weekly worship services, prayer is a priority, taking up a large chunk of the time. And I'm told Korean Christians tend to pray spontaneously and often. They believe and behave according to what's true: God really is omniscient. It's not surprising, then, that South Korea is one of the world's leaders in sending out missionaries. As our brothers and sisters in South Korea "pray continually" (1 Thessalonians 5:17), they are prompted to go and share Jesus.

It's tempting to lose heart when praying for non-believers if we can't see God clearly at work. But God invites us to be like the persistent widow and to always pray and never give up (Luke 18:1-8). You might find it helpful to keep a running list of people or communities to pray for so that you have a constant visual reminder. Or pray with a friend once a week for specific groups of people in your area. Or consider organizing a daily, weekly, or monthly prayer time for your whole church. Our church has continued to gather regularly to pray over Zoom in the evenings, even after the pandemic waned, because people found it easier after putting their kids to bed to pray quietly but corporately in their own homes. It doesn't matter how and where you pray, but that you are in fact praying.

It might be useful to think of praying for three main areas: for ourselves as believers, for the community we are trying to reach, and for God's glory to reign in our context. First, we must continually pray for ourselves so that we don't lose heart. Let's pray for boldness, watchfulness, and the willingness to make the most of our every opportunity (Ephesians 5:16) to love our neighbors and share Jesus with them. Then, we must pray continually for our communities because "the god of this age has blinded the minds of unbelievers, so that they cannot see the light of the gospel that displays the glory of Christ, who is the image of God" (2 Corinthians 4:4). And we must pray for God's glory to reign in our communities because our efforts are not physical but spiritual. As Paul reminds us, "Our struggle is not against flesh and blood, but against the rulers, against the authorities, against the powers of this dark world and against the spiritual forces of evil in the heavenly realms" (Ephesians 6:12).

We are totally dependent on the Holy Spirit to move in the hearts of those around us. By ourselves we cannot conjure up a revival of our cities or the salvation of even one person. God must do it. Let's cry out to him and ask him to move in our midst.

THEREFORE, GO!

After seeking to understand the felt needs of our communities and after devoting ourselves to prayer, we must go. Jesus says, "All authority in heaven and on earth has been given to me. Therefore go" (Matthew 28:18-19). We are called to be his witnesses all the way to the ends of the earth (Acts 1:8). And he has placed you and me precisely where we are so that all people might seek him and find him (Acts 17:26-27).

We have the calling, authority, and equipping of Jesus. Therefore, let's go. You may be wondering, though, where? To whom? The practical steps might feel paralyzing. Know this: wherever you are sitting right now is the frontline God has called you to. If Christ is in you, you are already there.

EXAMPLES IN ACTION

What follows are examples of churches around the globe welcoming outsiders way beyond Sunday. My hope is that these stories ignite in you a new vision and passion for missions in your midst.

Reaching College Students in the United States

A friend pastors a church in a college town. He and other leaders make a point of showing up at various festivals and rallies at the school with crates of ramen. They pass out the ramen, start conversations with the students, and invite them to church. College kids know their need for ramen but might not yet know their need for Jesus! Yet by God's grace, this church family seeks to become their home away from home so that they will meet Christ.

Providing Food in East Africa

When I asked a friend how her church in East Africa welcomes in the community around them, she said, "We don't have to try very hard. They come to us." She explained that felt needs for survival are strong in her community, and the people know that the church provides food and medicine, and help with bills when someone is in crisis. The church meets and worships in the open air, the people sing and display their joy for hours at a time, and newcomers trickle in looking for both material and spiritual nourishment.

Greeting Immigrants in Western Europe
One pastor friend in a large city in Western Europe told me that his church publishes a recommendation booklet for international migrants who are new to his metropolis. He said, "It gives recommendations for restaurants, markets, and parks. In a city that's extremely transient, it is an easy way for us to help serve the constant influx of new people in our neighborhoods." With the thoughtful gift of this booklet, his church members begin a relationship with newcomers who likely feel their need for connection and home. The church quickly becomes a place of belonging and care for new arrivals.

Welcoming Children in Japan
Japan is one of the world's most atheist nations. Those who follow Jesus number about one-half of one percent of the population.[22] Churches there must be excellent students of their culture and ask God to give them creativity as they seek to reach the lost. One church we know is led by both Japanese and American pastors (because of the sizable American military population). They know that the locals are curious about American

---

22 https://www.joshuaproject.net/countries/JA (accessed Apr. 8, 2022).

holidays and traditions, so they leverage that for Jesus. Before Halloween, church members canvas the neighborhood near the church building and invite children and families to come to their Harvest Festival. Hundreds of people turn out every year and play carnival-style games, hear live Christian music, and attend a gospel presentation. Everyone is invited back for the next big events—a Christmas play, an Easter-egg hunt, and a summertime Vacation Bible School.

Both Japanese and American church members serve at these events and are intentional about forming new friendships with the attendees. Local Japanese attendance increases every year. Now, after more than a decade of these rhythms, the church must provide all their materials in both English and Japanese, translators and translation radios at every event, and worship in both languages. Many Japanese people have come to Christ because of this persistent and faithful witness over many years. With joy and humility, our friend who has pastored this church for decades says, "God has given us great favor and fruit from [these events]."

Healing Marriages in Colorado
In my current community, people are educated, professional, and affluent. They do not lack material resources. What we noticed when we moved here, though, is that our neighbors lack connections. Families here tend to work hard, study hard, and play sports hard,

leaving almost no time for connection with one another or with other families. Seeking to meet felt relational needs, leaders in our church started a marriage ministry about one year ago. Couples in our church attend, and they invite their neighbors or friends to attend as well. Believers and non-believers gather for six weeks and receive hope and help for their marriages, as well as an introduction to Jesus and the healing he offers to both individuals and relationships.

WHAT YOU CAN WITH WHAT YOU HAVE

My friend Shanna is a missionary and pastor's wife in Prague, Czech Republic. She too served Ukrainian refugees as they fled west across Europe. With her kids and her friends, she prepared meals, made space in a hostel that her friend owns, and furnished a couple of flats loaned by residents of Prague to house refugees. Every time Shanna shared about their efforts on social media she said, "Do what you can, with what you have, where you are."[23]

Wherever you are right now, you are invited and empowered to share your life and the gospel with whoever is nearby. You don't need a strategic plan or year-end goal. You already have Christ in you, the hope of glory (Colossians 1:27). So simply "let your light shine

---

23 Theodore Roosevelt is well known for this motivating quote; https://www.theodorerooseveltcenter.org/Search?r=1&searchTerms=Do%20what%20you%20can,%20with%20what%20you%27ve%20got,%20where%20you%20are (accessed Apr. 15, 2022).

before others, that they may see your good deeds and glorify your Father in heaven" (Matthew 5:16).

The pressure is off. Jesus advances from you. The best days are ahead. Do what you can. With what you have. Where you are.

ACTION STEPS

Welcoming strangers into our lives and into our churches can feel overwhelming. You may feel too busy or too ill-equipped to take action. In reality, though, Jesus simply asks you to love people right where you are. Use the action steps below to help you think about how you might welcome others way beyond Sunday.

- *Identify what causes you fear when you think about loving the strangers in your community.* Butterfield suggests we fear that people will hurt us or that people will negatively influence our children or that we do not understand our world enough to be effective. Are you afraid of those things? What else would you add to the list? Take some time to share those fears with the Lord in prayer. Confess them to a fellow church member and commit to praying for freedom from those fears in the days ahead.

- *In a journal write down the answers to all the questions in the section above entitled "Know Your People Group."* Ask friends to help you with any blind spots you might have. Consult your city's or town's website or census information. Look for opportunities to talk to your actual neighbors and ask them about their lives.

- *Get out your day planner or open your calendar app on your phone.* Schedule one time each week for the next four weeks when you will actively pray for your community. Think about your physical neighbors, those who live near your church venue, your coworkers or fellow students, the people you see when you go grocery shopping, and the people who spend free time where you spend free time. Over the next month, ask the Lord to pursue and rescue these people.

- *Consider how and where you might go.* In response to Jesus' command to go, make a list of the people or groups of people in your life and community who do not yet know him. Brainstorm how you might share your life and the gospel with them. Share your brainstorm with a friend. Over the next few months look for opportunities to connect with and serve these people. Schedule a time with your friend in the near future when you will share how it's going.

6. SYSTEMS AND STRATEGIES FOR SUNDAY AND EVERY DAY

When my newly single mom and I first attended church, I was nine years old. My mom chose a church based on two things. First, her brother, whom she trusted, recommended a specific denomination. Second, there was a girl on my soccer team whose dad was a pastor. Her family extended a personal invitation to us to come to their church one Sunday—and it just happened to be in the recommended denomination. Given this uncanny coincidence, my mom decided to give my teammate's church a try.

I marvel and even now tear up whenever I think about it. I was a little girl in an unbelieving family, walking through the trauma of divorce and the turbulence of two homes rather than one. I do not come from a great Christian heritage of a rich spiritual legacy.

But the kindness of a teammate's family in inviting us to church changed my life and my eternity. I was lost, but then I was found. Jesus saw us, and he had mercy.

He led us to himself through the generous hospitality of another little girl and her family. It blows me away to think that I heard the gospel there and believed. I made a public profession of faith a couple years later and boldly asked to be baptized, alone, on stage in front of that welcoming congregation. It makes no worldly sense, but I've belonged to my Father in heaven ever since.

THE HOLY SPIRIT, OUR SPIRIT, AND OUR SYSTEM

A welcoming church is first a work of the Holy Spirit. In and of ourselves we are self-focused people. Our flesh impels us to accommodate ourselves, not to go out of our way to welcome others in. As Christ-followers, we are dependent on the Holy Spirit to create in us a desire to make space for others. What a gift to have the Helper living in us, who is faithful to do this good work (John 14:16). He is forming us more and more into the image of Jesus every day (2 Corinthians 3:17-18). So, if your church is already a welcoming church, praise the Lord! He has done this. If you are someone who loves to invite others in, praise the Lord! He has done this.

As we Christians display the spirit of welcome that the Spirit has given us, we spur one another on to do likewise (Hebrews 10:24). Welcoming begets welcoming. Hospitality begets hospitality. Generosity begets generosity. A welcoming atmosphere in our churches grows by contagion.

I mentioned Jaimie and Kenton in chapter 1. They are the young couple who make every effort every Sunday to welcome newcomers in. When other church members see what Jaimie and Kenton are doing, they do it too. It spreads from one church member to the next. A hospitable spirit rises among us. It's a work of God, and it's a gift.

The Holy Spirit is pre-eminent. Without his work in us, we are without hope. And yet, while creating a church culture of welcome is Spirit-driven, it does not negate the need for systems. We need systems in place so that we can intentionally and even methodically welcome newcomers in the front door and—through the gospel—into deep, authentic community.

The idea of creating strategies and systems may feel cold to you. Providing such structures may feel like the opposite of being Spirit-led. But creating these practical means and methods allows us to be *better welcomers*. It's like pursuing a spiritual discipline. It's a way to ensure that we are accomplishing a work that God has already called us to and equipped us to do. Without such structures, we tend to get lazy or distracted and go off-mission.

This chapter is not meant to be prescriptive. Instead, it's meant to help us think through the systems (or lack thereof) we have in our lives and churches, and whether we are serving visitors and potential newcomers well. This is a chance to get practical and examine the nuts and bolts of our specific communities. As we saw in the last chapter, each church is in a specific setting, each of which warrants a specific kind of welcome. May this chapter allow us to check our own work and improve upon what we're already doing.

And as we move forward in faith, let's remember two things. First, Jesus will build his church (Matthew 16:18). That's a promise from the mouth of Christ himself, and he will keep it. The pressure is off you and me. And second, let us, as Paul says, "strenuously contend with all the energy Christ so powerfully works in [us]" (Colossians 1:29). Making space for everyone requires strenuous labor—but that labor should be done with the energy that Christ supplies. Brothers and sisters, let us work by the power of Jesus for his name and his renown. May we rest in him and be moved by him as we seek to welcome others into a relationship with him.

MAKE IT EASY

Multiple barriers make it difficult for visitors to walk into a church for the first time. In some places around the world, worshiping the risen Jesus is illegal, and visiting church means gathering in a secret location after nightfall. In some cities throughout the cultural West, religion and church attendance are so frowned upon that visiting a church might cost relationships, professional advancement, and respect in the community. Perhaps the greatest barrier in Western culture, though, is apathy. People are both self-sufficient and busy. In the modern West most people don't *feel* a need for religion. We often don't rely on the church to meet our material needs—medical care, food, or shelter. Nor do we see ourselves as having many spiritual needs—we tend to view ourselves as good people, and so, if there is a god, he or she probably thinks we're fine. Additionally, people are simply busy. They fill their calendars with work, recreation, travel, and leisure. Making space for religious practices throughout the week just doesn't cross their minds.

While long-time Christians might feel that church attendance is second nature, most people don't feel that way. For most of our friends, neighbors, and colleagues, going to church is weird. Imagine a setting where you have never been: a casino, a biker gang's clubhouse, a mosque, a Jewish synagogue, or a Shinto shrine. Now imagine being invited to enter in. Imagine how uncomfortable and foolish you would feel. What would it take to put you at ease?

The systems in our churches, then, should seek to make the culturally difficult task of visiting church as easy as possible. To practice hospitality well, we must strive to remove barriers, awkwardness, or embarrassment.

But first, a caveat: church attendance will always appear foolish in the world's eyes. Paul tells us that God chose the foolish things of the world to shame the wise, the weak things to shame the strong, and the lowly things so that no one may boast in him or herself, but in God alone

Jen Oshman

(1 Corinthians 1:26-31). The gospel is only attractive to those who admit they are lost, broken, and in need of rescue. I'm not suggesting that we make visiting a church so convenient and attractive that we demolish the gospel. But I am encouraging us to remember what it's like to be an outsider and to do all we can to open wide our doors.

Let's look at our lives and our churches through those eyes. Ask yourself: If I were going to a setting that was completely new and foreign to me, what would help me walk through the doors? What would make me feel more welcome than weird? Let's envision some of the steps required for a nonattender to make it to church.

A Personal Invitation
By far the best way to help someone visit a church is to personally invite them and accompany them to your worship services or events. My friend Rachel lives in Paris and longs for her international neighbors to know Jesus as Lord and Savior. She consistently hosts supper clubs, book clubs, game nights, and coffees in her apartment for her neighbors, who hail from around France, Italy, Vietnam, the US, and Portugal. The relationships formed at such gatherings over time make it organic and easy for her to then invite her friends to her church. Rachel is neither secretive nor subtle about her faith. Her neighbors find out she's a follower of Jesus quickly after they meet her. She says they do find her unusual and maybe even weird, but the constant care she displays for her neighbors draws them in. So her eventual invitation to church isn't

weird—it's the overflow of the friendship that already exists. When they accept, she brings them with her on Sunday, and she trusts the Lord to move in their hearts according to his will. Who might you invite to church? Write a name or two in the margin here and start praying about and planning your personal invitation.

Your Digital Front Door
In the 21st century, our churches' front doors are online. Most people visit the digital location of anywhere they go before they visit the physical location. Does your church's website make it easy for a digital visitor to take the next, physical step? Does the website clearly state your location and service times and what visitors can expect? (For example, usual attire, children's ministry offerings, parking limitations, and anything else you can think of!) Also, double check that your website is written in plain language that is easily understood by a non-believer. We Christians slip into using "Christianese" more than we like to admit.

Having covered the basics, there's still more we can do. My husband was recently revamping our church's website, and he sought out the wisdom of a marketing firm. I'll pass along one enlightening suggestion they had for us. They said that a church's website should convey how the church might tangibly help a potential visitor. In other words, to return to the theme of chapter 5, the felt needs of our communities should be reflected on our website. People who visit church websites are wondering if our faith families have anything to offer them personally. They want to read stories and see examples of how our institution might intersect with their everyday needs.

This advice helped my own church to rethink what we post online. We have more work to do, but rather than posting *only* logistics, programs, and doctrines, we realize we need to share human stories so that online visitors can identify with real attendees.

Every church member can help with this endeavor by posting a review of their church online through Facebook, Yelp, Google, or any relevant platform. Share your own story about how your church meets you right where you are, that others may be drawn in.

Sunday-Morning Systems

Theologian and author Rebecca McLaughlin says, "An alone person in our gatherings is an emergency."[24] She and her husband have made a rule for themselves that anytime they see someone alone at their worship services, they must stop what they're doing and go chat with or sit next to that person. She says, "Friends can wait for our attention on a Sunday. Better still, they can mobilize in mission too. Spurring each other on to welcome strangers in Christ's name won't weaken our friendships; it will deepen them."[25]

---

24 https://www.desiringgod.org/articles/make-sunday-mornings-uncomfortable (accessed Apr. 12, 2022).

25 https://www.desiringgod.org/articles/make-sunday-mornings-uncomfortable

This is a needed exhortation for all church members and a useful principle to apply to everything we do on Sunday mornings. The principle that an alone person is an emergency likely prompts us to have greeters at our front doors, an information table or place to go with questions, maybe ushers or escorts that guide new families to appropriate worship spaces and classrooms, and plenty of signage, as well as people who stand ready to help anyone who looks like they're not sure where to go or what to do.

While these nuts and bolts might seem like the concern of church leaders only, it's good for church attendees to be aware of these systems too. If we all know the purpose of these practical measures, then we can all get on board and help. Church leaders cannot do the welcoming work alone—in fact, they often cannot do it at all on a Sunday morning because they are preoccupied with things like sound checks, ensuring classrooms are staffed with volunteers, and surprises like flooding toilets or leaking roofs.

If in the last chapter we said, "Every member a missionary", in this chapter we're saying, "Every member a greeter". Both systems ("official" greeters and information tables, for example) and organic culture (church attendees who eagerly go out of their way to welcome others) are needed.

(accessed Apr. 12, 2022).

Make Connections

Expanding on McLaughlin's rule above, let's go beyond the temporary connection we make with visitors on Sunday mornings and make sure we foster longer-term connections right away. As humans we are made for connection and community. We all want to know others and to be known. It can feel scary or silly to begin a conversation with a visitor, but it's worth it!

Because of our role in missions, I get the chance to regularly meet people in churches all over the world. I often ask new friends, "What brought you to this church?" Or "Tell me how you got involved here at this church". Most often they tell me something like "The first Sunday we visited someone asked us out to lunch, and we've been coming back ever since". Or "My first time here I exchanged phone numbers with someone, and we've been friends ever since". Or "I was immediately invited into a small group so I got connected to a group of friends, and now this is my family".

The desire to connect is universal. And connections begin with that first, sometimes scary conversation. In the family of God, strangers can become siblings. Sunday-morning systems—like ensuring these first conversations are the norm—play a key role in making space for everyone.

Further into the Family

As you think about your specific faith family, what milestones or checkpoints would enable someone to progress from being a stranger to becoming a sibling? In your setting, what are the means of moving someone further into the family?

A church near us hosts lunch once a month for newcomers to join in after the worship service and get to know church leaders. A church in Asia plans quarterly church-wide dinners where everyone is placed into a group that gathers for dinner at the home of a volunteer host. This allows the whole church to gather on the same evening, but in intimate groups around the community where people get to know one another more deeply. A church in Europe matches those who are interested with others in groups of two or three for weekly meetings of encouragement and mutual discipleship. Our family hosts a six-week small group three times a year to which we invite newcomers to get a taste of what it's like to join a small group at our church. This allows them to get to know the pastor's family and have an idea of the benefits and responsibilities of joining a small group before they make the commitment. Many churches offer membership classes and one-on-one meetings with elders to help identify the newcomers' gifts and needs.

There's no one right way to encourage strangers to become siblings. Each context calls for creativity, the power of the Holy Spirit, and the intentional follow-through of existing church members. Our role is to be faithful to welcome others in. And the Lord himself will build his church.

Technological Tips

When I reached out to pastors to ask them about their systems on Sundays, many suggested things I had never thought of! Some of the ideas were technological. For example, one church puts a QR code on the back of every chair in their sanctuary so that everyone can easily access information on Sunday mornings. Many churches use physical and digital "Connect Cards," through which visitors can share their contact information or prayer needs. One church has a video camera in their lobby. At the weekly staff meeting they watch the video so that the whole staff can see the faces of visitors, learn names, and share information that will help them welcome the visitors back. Lots of churches employ apps and databases to exchange visitors' names, log attendance, and keep track of which leaders are caring for new and regular attendees, while following government regulation and data protection.

It's well worth reaching out to those you know in other churches and asking them what they or their churches do. We can learn some of the best tips and "tricks of the trade" from others.

A BALANCED PERSPECTIVE

There are two ditches we can fall into when thinking about using systems to open wide our church doors. One ditch is thinking that systems are crass and leave no room for our faith or the movement of the Holy Spirit. The other ditch is to rely wholeheartedly on the systems and think about our churches as businesses and attendees as customers.

With God's help we can avoid both ditches. At once, we can be faithful and intentional about employing good systems that help us fulfill our God-given mission. And we must remain humble, aware that Jesus alone can woo people to himself. May we be in awe of our Lord whenever he brings a new sibling into the family, and may we thank him for using us in the process.

Nine-year-old me and my single mom benefited greatly from the practical strategies of that first church we attended. Their emphasis on extending personal invitations brought us in the door. I vividly remember feeling very awkward and different. But I also remember the warmth of the welcome. All kinds of people shook our hands and asked about our story. I went to children's Sunday school and had the sweetest teachers. Mr. Tilsley helped me memorize the Lord's prayer right away. Ms. Connie invited me to be in the kids' musical. Humanly speaking, it was the kindness of God's people, plus their intentional systems, that made us, who were once strangers, into their siblings through faith in Christ.

ACTION STEPS

Whether you are a church leader or a relatively new attendee, this chapter is for you. If our churches are going to display genuine warmth and welcome, we need all hands on deck. How can you help?

- *Commit to seeing an alone person on Sunday as an emergency.* Make it a point each week to pursue anyone who looks new or unsure.

- *Try to regularly sit with new people in the pews on Sunday morning.* It's easy to get into a rut or feel we must only sit with our biological family members each week. But the faith family is bigger than that. Display that reality by regularly sitting with different people in different places.

- *Think about a formal role you could play in welcoming people to your church.* Reach out to your church leaders and ask if you can help greet or usher. Or offer your help during the week with maintaining visitor databases, or with following up newcomers with offers of help or an invitation to coffee or the next church event.

7. OUTWARD
AND ONWARD

I'll never forget one Sunday morning after our family had just landed back in the US after living overseas. Before we perceived that the Lord was calling us to plant a new church in Colorado, we had to find a place to worship. "Church shopping," as it's sometimes called, was tough for many reasons. But on that particular Sunday morning, I witnessed something that caused me to be downright giddy: curled-up linoleum in the women's bathroom.

A worn-out restroom would not normally give me joy, but the somewhat neglected flooring told me something important about that church. Combined with a crowd bustling in the sanctuary, the lively conversations that ensued as soon as the worship service ended, and the gospel-packed sermon that we had just listened to, it was obvious that this church had a healthy outward focus. As first-time visitors we were greeted by the pastor, other church staff, and everyone sitting near us in the sanctuary. Volunteers met my kids at the Sunday-school room door with huge smiles, and our pewmates offered me tissues when I shed some tears during the service. These people cared more about welcoming newcomers than they did about the bathroom floors. Their heart and their budget were set more on people than their facility.

I'm not suggesting that curled linoleum is a litmus test for faithful churches. But we had visited at least a few churches that had beautiful bathrooms but no obvious enthusiasm for newcomers or the grace and gospel of Jesus. Seeing those vibrant people and their service, alongside an imperfect building, gave me hope that this congregation would be a place of refuge in our transition—a people who would make space for us.

And that initial assessment was right. After a couple Sundays, a handful of conversations with church members, and even invitations to hang out with them during the week, we learned that this church's regular rhythm was to multiply. They routinely sent out new pastors who had been trained in-house, along with teams made up of their own members, to plant new churches around the city of Denver and the state of Colorado.

My husband and I asked how this could be, as we had observed multiple packed worship services. How was this congregation so full—and so full of life—if they were constantly sending people out? We learned that every time the congregation commissions a new church plant, the gaps left behind in people and leaders are quickly filled again by newcomers. With each plant the population of the sending church decreases, then rises, and the cycle repeats. One pastor on staff explained that it seems like people in the community, including those who have never before been to church, are constantly drawn in by the energy and excitement within their congregation. It is counterintuitive, to be sure. But over the few months that we worshipped with that church, we saw it happen right before our eyes.

The question we'll consider in this chapter is: how does a church build—and maintain—that sort of momentum?

THAT IRRESISTIBLE INWARD PULL

The church that our family planted along with several other families just celebrated its fifth birthday. We threw a party complete with dinner and dancing to rejoice. Those of us who were there in our church's very first days in our living room kept looking at each other with mouths open and eyes wide: "Can you believe we actually made it?"

We were thrilled to be five years old in a community where 65% of the population claim to have no religious beliefs, and only 17% claim to be evangelical Christians.[26] Having lived in two of the most atheistic nations in the world, I know those numbers may seem high to you, depending on where you live. But I assure you, they are

---

26 http://www.city-data.com/city/Parker-Colorado.html (accessed May 11, 2022).

low compared to the rest of the United States. Colorado and the west are considered dry soil for the gospel, so five years felt worth the party!

For every ten church plants in the United States, three to four don't make it to year four.[27] This reality can easily pull church-planting teams and pastors inward, to an unhealthy self-focus. Those early months and years are full of uncertainty. *Will anyone show up this week? Will there be enough people to staff the kids' rooms? Will people tithe enough to cover the bills?* If church-planting teams aren't careful, they can fixate on survival rather than the glory of God and the good of their community.

Established churches are not immune from this irresistible inward pull either. The numbers are hard to pin down, but the most optimistic estimate is that about 3,700 churches close their doors each year in the United States; more pessimistic estimations are 6,000-10,000.[28] In the United Kingdom, research shows that over 2,000 churches have closed in the last ten years, bringing the number of open churches down to 39,800 from 42,000.[29] Any number of closing churches

---

27 E. Stetzer and W. Bird (2008), "The State of Church Planting in the United States: Research Overview and Qualitative Study of Primary Church Planting Entities", *Journal of the American Society for Church Growth*, 19(2), 1-42; Retrieved from https://place.asburyseminary.edu/jascg/vol19/iss2/2/ (accessed May 11, 2022).

28 https://research.lifeway.com/2018/01/16/hope-for-dying-churches/ (accessed May 11, 2022).

29 https://evangelicalfocus.com/europe/14005/uk-over-2000-churches-closed-in-the-last-10-years (accessed May 21, 2022).

can feel daunting to pastors and church members, especially if they observe their own congregations shrinking. It's understandable that church leaders are tempted to circle the wagons to protect themselves and their congregations.

But does that work? Does an inward focus preserve a church? The counterintuitive answer is no. An inward focus harms a church, while an outward focus brings life.

THE EYEBROW-RAISING TRUTH

Author and pastor Tim Keller founded Redeemer City to City, an organization that has helped plant over 700 churches in over 75 cities around the globe. Keller says, "The vigorous, continual planting of new congregations is the single most crucial strategy for (1) the numerical growth of the body of Christ in a city and (2) the continual corporate renewal and revival of the existing churches in a city ... This is an eyebrow-raising statement, but to those who have done any study at all, it is not even controversial."[30] Evidence shows that when churches set out to plant more churches, it's actually good for the mother (or sending or planting) church. Intuition says churches should hunker down and focus inward if they want to be healthy, but the very opposite is true. Churches that maintain an outward focus are the healthiest.

---

30 Tim Keller, *Why Plant Churches?* Redeemer City to City, January 1, 2002; https://redeemercitytocity.com/articles-stories/why-plant-churches (accessed May 12, 2022).

Thom Rainer is a researcher and church expert who has studied and written extensively about church health. While not speaking about church planting per se, Rainer observes a similar phenomenon. He says, "The most common factor in declining churches is an inward focus. The ministries are only for the members. The budgetary funds are used almost exclusively to meet the needs of the members. The times of worship and worship styles are geared primarily for the members. Conflict takes place when members don't get things their way. You get the picture."[31]

Whether a church's inward focus prevents it from planting new churches or from seeking to minister to the community outside its walls, an inward focus is always to the church's peril. An inward focus is deadly while an outward focus produces life, both for that local church and the larger kingdom beyond.

LOSING OUR (CHURCH) LIVES TO SAVE THEM

This reality shouldn't surprise us. While our flesh, intuition, and sometimes even church culture naturally tell us to turn inward, this gravitational pull is counter to the call of Christ. Jesus says, "For whoever wants to save their life will lose it, but whoever loses their life for me and for the gospel will save it" (Mark 8:35).

---

31 Thom Rainer, "The Most Common Factor In Declining Churches", Lifeway Research, August 16, 2016; https://research.lifeway.com/2016/08/16/the-most-common-factor-in-declining-churches/ (accessed May 12, 2022).

We know this to be true on an individual level. We who have surrendered to Jesus understand that our Lord has asked us to forsake life on our own terms and to live by his strength (not our own) and for his glory (not our own). Yet this spiritual reality applies not just to our own individual lives but to our corporate church lives as well. To the extent that we try to save, or preserve, or protect our churches for their own sakes, we will lose them. Jesus says to you and me and to every church family, *Lose your life for me and for the gospel and that's where you will find true life*.

This spiritual reality is what my family observed at the church with the curled-up linoleum in the bathroom. Their priorities were evident: fixing up their own church home came second to multiplying more church homes out in the community. One might think they needed to keep their facilities pristine so that more people would visit and come back. It would certainly be a bonus for the church members who use that bathroom week in and week out. And please hear me, I'm not making a prescription for all churches to neglect their buildings for the sake of the gospel. But this church's example is provoking and worth considering. In general, do we invest more time, money, and energy inwardly or outwardly?

Whether it's in church-planting or in strategically serving the community beyond ourselves, we do have to relinquish precious resources. But doing so doesn't kill us or even harm us. Yes, the "gospel goodbyes" are painful when we send church-planters and people out. And the outward-focused investments require each church member to sacrifice. Change is hard, to be sure. There is a real cost. But each time we regroup, we build up again, and we go out again.

Knowing that an inward focus is deadly, church leaders and members are wise to keep an eye out for signs that their churches are too self-focused. Here are some questions worth asking:

- Does your congregation see the culture outside your church as an enemy to be kept away or as people to be welcomed in with the love and mercy of Jesus?

- Are your church attendees more likely to ask, "What can I receive?" or "What can I give?" Are they consumers or contributors?

- When presented with a plan to plant a new church or to provide a missional outreach activity, is your congregation excited or resistant?

- Does your congregation tend to idolize the past and the "good ol' days" or is there a fresh excitement about what God is doing today?

- Looking at your church budget and church calendar, do you see evidence of spending time and money on outward-facing ministry?

- As a pastor or church leader, do you feel tempted to view people in the pews as dollars in the bank, thereby making yourself susceptible to catering to the people "in here" at the expense of the souls "out there"?

If we're honest, I think every Christian can detect in themselves an element of self-focus. Even the most missional Christian grows weary. I am aware of a light that appears on the dashboard of my own soul when I become inward focused. When I begin to compare my own ministry to that of others' and I think I am doing more for the kingdom than they are, I know I have slipped into a selfish and inward way of thinking about my kingdom work. The light on the dashboard lets me know that I'm playing a lethal comparison game and that my eyes are fixed inward, on myself, and not outward on my Lord and his people. Thankfully, our God is endless in mercy, and he will help us. May you and I look to the cross for a renewed perspective and a revived motivation to lay ourselves down again and again for others, as our Savior did for us.

THE CHURCH IS PLAN A

Maybe it's because I've been involved in missions and church-planting for a long time, but I have heard many pastors claim, "The church is Plan A for reaching the world, and there is no Plan B!" Maybe you've heard that too. Maybe it's a cliché. But no matter how many times I hear or read this phrase, it sobers me anew.

This life is not a dress rehearsal. I have one life, and the Lord Jesus has asked me to lay it down for him and the gospel. Am I really doing that? As a church leader, do I lead people toward true life? Or am I satisfied with safety, comfort, and the path of least resistance? Even as I write these words, I whisper a quiet prayer that the Holy Spirit will give me a fresh desire to make him known in my community and an unending drive to make space in the church for everyone.

After Jesus' resurrection from the dead, but before he ascended to heaven, he gave his followers the Great Commission: "All authority in heaven and on earth has been given to me. Therefore go and make disciples of all nations, baptizing them in the name of the Father and of the Son and of the Holy Spirit, and teaching them to obey everything I have commanded you. And surely I am with you always, to the very end of the age" (Matthew 28:18-20). In addition to these instructions, he promised to help them, saying, "You will receive power when the Holy Spirit comes on you; and you will be my witnesses in Jerusalem, and in all Judea and Samaria, and to the ends of the earth" (Acts 1:8).

Based on Jesus' authority and by the power of the Holy Spirit, you and I and every Christian have been called to a life of outward living. The gospel moves onward, and the kingdom grows *bigger because of the church*. We are entrusted with the task of proclaiming Christ, being his witnesses, and baptizing and teaching his new followers.

This is Plan A, and there is no Plan B!

The early church at Antioch, where the followers of Jesus were first called Christians (Acts 11:26), gives us an exciting example of what this outward focus looks like. The Christians there actively shared the gospel with both Jews and Gentiles in their community (v 19-20), while also maintaining rigorous discipleship inside the church (v 22-26). The Christians were generous and eager to offer help and mercy to those in need (v 27-30). And their international leadership (a sign of outward focus itself, as the church did not limit itself to one ethnicity) sent two out of five of their leaders on a missionary journey to proclaim Christ beyond their borders (Acts 13:1-5).

The church at Antioch quite literally changed the world and changed history as the message of Jesus spread from there around the globe and through the ages. In heaven I look forward to thanking these siblings in Christ from Antioch for their outward focus. I know they will say it was for their joy, and I will reply that it was also for my eternal good.

BIG-K OR LITTLE-K KINGDOM

We have a pastor friend in Denver who—with a big grin on his face—sometimes says to his congregation, "Let's grow some fruit on other churches' trees." He's inviting his congregation to give money or time or service to other churches in the city. He doesn't want his flock to focus on themselves but to always look outward, at the broader body of Christ. He often says, "I'm not interested in growing our little-k kingdom. I want to grow the big-K Kingdom." As a result, his congregation is excited to serve both at home and outside their own community. They have missionaries around the globe, ministries all over the metro area, and a growing faith family themselves. It's a joy to see the name of that church pop up around town, as it inevitably does, for their role in homeless ministries, pregnancy-resource centers, foster care, and more.

And the "curled-up linoleum" church? They started a whole church-planting network. That one congregation had so much joy and success in planting new churches that they started a ministry to support others to do the same. Their vision is to make Jesus nonignorable in Denver and to the ends of the earth. Over the last six years or so they have planted or revitalized 27 churches. Their tenacious outward focus has not only grown the big-K Kingdom, but it has made their own faith family healthy and joyful as well.

So then, outward and onward, brothers and sisters. For God's glory, for our own good, and for the joy of all who might know Jesus.

ACTION STEPS
Having an outward focus as a church family leads to growth—both for that local congregation and for the

Big-K Kingdom. Consider how you and your church can increasingly "look out" in order to welcome others in.

- *Look at your calendar or day-planner from the last year.* How do your inward-facing commitments compare to your outward-facing commitments? How do you feel like you are doing with the command to "love your neighbor as yourself" (Mark 12:31) when it comes to your time? Consider this for yourself, your family, and your church.

- *Look at your financial budget from the last year.* How do your inward-facing expenses compare to your outward-facing expenses? How do you feel like you are doing with the command to "love your neighbor as yourself" (Mark 12:31) when it comes to your money? Consider this for yourself, your family, and your church.

- *If you feel like you personally, or your family, falls short in outward-facing ministry, brainstorm a list of things you could do to minister to your community.* Plan one event right now. It doesn't have to be complicated. You could invite neighbors you don't know yet over for dinner, sign up to help in your city's free food pantry, or call the local pregnancy-resource center and see if you could come help organize donated baby items. Whatever you decide, put it on the calendar right now.

- *If you feel like your church falls short in outward-facing ministry, create a list of ways your church body could better "see" the community outside your walls.* Pray about how you might initiate that ministry. Meet with a church leader or two and offer your ideas and commit your own efforts and time for the task and invite others to join in.

- *Pray and ask the Lord to help you apply the same love you have for yourself and your own family and church family to those outside your home and church.* Ask God to show you tangible ways you can love your neighbors as you love yourself.

CONCLUSION

As those who have been welcomed into the family of Jesus, we look forward to the fulfillment of John's vision of heaven, recorded in the book of Revelation:

There before me was a great multitude that no one could count, from every nation, tribe, people and language, standing before the throne and before the Lamb. They were wearing white robes and were holding palm branches in their hands. And they cried out in a loud voice: "Salvation belongs to our God, who sits on the throne, and to the Lamb." (Revelation 7:9-10)

Can you picture it? A crowd so big you can't even begin to count all the people. The diversity of every single nation, tribe, people, and language all in one place. And all of us crying out in unified worship to our one true God. Such overwhelming and beautiful unity in diversity!

Our global faith family grows every day. According to his good will and in his perfect time, our Father in heaven keeps adding brothers and sisters to our numbers from all over the globe. He adds to the church through the witness of the church.

Your own local church is evidence of this. Your local faith family—in all its diversity and complexity and fun and ease, and even as it stretches and tries you and requires your patience—is a beautiful expression of God's family right in your own community. As different and as quirky and unique as we each may be, in Christ we are family.

And one day—no one knows which day or which hour—Jesus will return, and our family will be complete.

Sharing Christ in our post-Christian context is daunting. As you read each chapter of this book and prayed through each action step, my guess is that you felt anticipation and excitement, as well as some fear and sense of being overwhelmed. Let's ask the Lord of the harvest to send us out to our neighbors and other nations, full of faith and expectant about what he will do. And let's get ready to welcome those people in to hear, and, we pray, receive the gospel, asking the Lord to help us love one another well. Let's ask him to fill us with unconditional and persevering love for one another. Let's ask him to make us good and beautiful and true siblings to our fellow believers, right here, inside the church.

Here is a truth I return to again and again, which is immensely helpful to me: *God calls me to be faithful, but it is he who must be fruitful.* This truth has comforted me, and empowered me, as I've imperfectly shared Christ on three different continents for over two decades and sought to be a faithful sister and welcoming church member in whatever faith family God has placed me. Let me explain.

The Scriptures are full of commands to share God's love with others. We have seen those commands throughout this book. Love God and love others. Be ambassadors for Christ. Go and baptize disciples and teach the nations about Jesus. Be Christ's witnesses in Judea, Samaria, and to the ends of the earth. There's no doubt that we are commanded by God to shine brightly in our generation, that he may be known.

But while we are called to shine, it is God alone who provides the growth. Paul says, "I planted the seed, Apollos watered it, but God has been making it grow. So neither the one who plants nor the one who waters is anything, but only God, who makes things grow" (1 Corinthians 3:6-7). By all means, let's give our lives over to the task of planting seeds and watering them. Let us be faithful witnesses, porch lights in a dark night. May God use you and me to reveal himself to many more sons and daughters in his family. But let us remember too that "no one can come to [Jesus] unless the Father who sent [him] draws them" (John 6:44).

We must be faithful to God's call on us to be ambassadors and witnesses. But it's only God who saves. We must be faithful to God's call on us to love one another well. But it's only God who can enable us to lay ourselves down for each other. We are not God. But let us long to be and pray to be church members who represent him well. Church members who make space for everyone—both those on the inside and those we have yet to welcome in from the outside.

May we go out with boldness and joy and freedom and lightness of heart. We are required to be faithful, empowered by the Holy Spirit, and compelled by the grace of Jesus. But we are not required to save souls ourselves. The growth of the church is not on you.

Jesus alone says, "I will build my church, and the gates of Hades will not overcome it" (Matthew 16:18). The church will grow. The celebration and worship John recorded in Revelation will happen. All of history is hurtling toward that vision. It will come to pass, whatever our imperfections.

Our God is sovereign and good, and he has a glorious plan. The church is his Plan A, and we are invited on the adventure. Will we accept his invitation? Will we plant the seeds and water them? Will we make space for everyone? By his grace and for his glory, let it be. Brothers and sisters, let's do all we can—as we trust and hope in God alone—to welcome others in.

DISCUSSION GUIDE
FOR SMALL GROUPS

1. HOW JESUS WELCOMES US

1. Can you remember walking into your church (or a church) for the first time? How did it feel? What were your fears and first impressions?

Read Philippians 2:5-11

2. Trace out the different steps Jesus took to welcome us into God's family. Which verse or phrase are you particularly struck by?

3. What might it look like for us, in our relationships with one another, to forsake our status, become a servant, and humble ourselves as Jesus did?

4. In contrast, what might it look like to hold on to our status, serve ourselves, and walk proudly?

5. What comfort is there in these verses, and in this chapter, for when we're feeling convicted about the ways in which we've fallen short in welcoming others?

2. THE RADICAL WELCOME OF THE EARLY CHURCH

1. Imagine that this Sunday, 3,000 new believers are added to your church. What would you do next?

On the day of Pentecost, about 3,000 people accepted the apostles' message and were baptized (Acts 2:41); previously, there were around 120 believers (1:15).

Read Acts 2:42-47

2. What actions and attitudes marked this new Christian community? How did they relate to God and to one another?

3. Why is this all the more remarkable, given what we're told in verses 5-11? Where did the power to live in this way come from?

4. What was the effect of this distinctive gospel community (v 47)?

The growth of the church didn't stop there. This chapter explored how the early church welcomed people of all ethnicities, all classes, and of both sexes into God's community through the gospel.

5. How do you think your church is doing on each of those fronts? Where is there room to grow?

6. What about on a personal level? Are there ways in which you tend to gravitate towards people like yourself at church? What could you do differently?

3. THIS CHURCH OPENS WIDE HER DOORS

1. Think about some of the non-churchgoers you know. What impression do you think they have of Christians and of the church in general?

Read Mark 2:13-17

2. What had the Pharisees got wrong about Jesus and about themselves? What had the tax collectors and sinners perceived rightly?

3. Why is it sometimes easy to forget that we too are sick people in need of a doctor?

4. If we think of ourselves as sinners in Jesus' hospital, how will that shape our attitude to the needy people we encounter?

5. Imagine someone coming to your church for the first time. What signals would they get that your church is "a hospital for sinners, not a museum for saints" (p 48)?

6. "If you have eyes to see it, there are likely many people in your church who are extending [a] welcome to the broken and needy" (p 53). Who in your church family is doing this already? Praise God for them!

4. WELCOME TO THE FAMILY

1. Think back to when you joined your church. How long did it take before you really felt part of the family? How easy do you think it is for a believer joining your church to feel at home?

Read Mark 10:25-30

2. What's remarkable about Jesus' promise here?

"Jesus gives us a new definition of 'family' ... The temporary families that we are born into and marry into are superseded by the eternal family we have in Christ" (p 62).

3. Are there any ways in which you're in danger of prioritizing your earthly family at the expense of your spiritual family? Why is that, do you think?

4. Pages 65-66 talk about two groups of people in a church: those who get too cozy in the "in-crowd" and those who are looking for a sense of intimacy but feel on the edge. Do either of those describe you?

5. This chapter encourages us to commit to a local church, submit to its leaders, and minister to one another (p 66-68). How will doing each of those things help a person's church to feel like family?

6. What's one thing that you could do this month to help newcomers feel part of your church family?

5. WELCOMING WAY BEYOND SUNDAY

1. "If you're a Christian, you're a missionary" (p 77). Do you agree that many of us are held back from that by fear (p 78)? What are your particular fears in this area?

Read Matthew 5:14-16

2. How do Jesus' words encourage and excite you in the face of that fear?

3. This chapter talked about three tasks before us as missionaries to our community. Work through each of them in turn:

   a) *Know your community*. Get a big piece of paper and map out your answers to the questions on pages 79-80, along with anything else that seems relevant. Identify any gaps in your knowledge too—what more information do you require in order to truly understand the needs of particular groups?

   b) *Pray*. With your mind map in front of you, spend time in prayer for the people, groups, and needs you've discussed. You could start by reading 2 Corinthians 4:4-6 together.

   c) *Go*. As a group, plan to do one thing together that will help you to engage with and serve members of your community.

6. SYSTEMS AND STRATEGIES FOR SUNDAY AND EVERY DAY

1. When did you last speak to a new person in church? Describe the encounter and how it made you feel.

Read Colossians 1:25-29

2. What do these verses reveal about how Paul viewed gospel ministry?

3. What implications are there for us as we think about welcoming others to hear the gospel at our church?

Remember, "while creating a church culture of welcome is Spirit-driven, it does not negate the need for systems. We need systems in place so that we can intentionally and even methodically welcome newcomers in the front door and—through the gospel—into deep, authentic community" (p 93).

4. "Multiple barriers make it difficult for visitors to walk into a church for the first time" (p 94). What are some of the barriers getting in the way for people in your local community, do you think? How could you help make it easier?

5. What do you think of the idea that "an alone person in our gatherings is an emergency" (p 98)? How would your church gatherings change if you took that seriously?

7. OUTWARD AND ONWARD

1. What causes churches to become inward-looking, do you think?

2. Look at the list of questions on pages 112-113. Where do you see warning signs that you yourself might be tending towards self-focus?

Read Mark 8:31-35

3. In what sense did Jesus reject the temptation towards self-preservation (v 31-33)?

4. What does following after him as his disciple involve (v 34-35)?

Read Acts 11:19-30

5. In what different ways were the believers in Antioch and in Jerusalem outward-looking? What fruit did this result in?

6. "The church is Plan A for reaching the world, and there is no Plan B!" (p 113). How does that excite you or challenge you?

7. Look at the action steps on pages 116-118. How might you and your church invest in growing the "big-K Kingdom," not just your "little-k kingdom"?

RESOURCES FOR SMALL GROUPS

Access the free small group kit at loveyourchurchseries. com. The free kit includes a video introduction to each session, as well as downloadable PDFs of a discussion guide and worksheets. Each session is based on a chapter of the book.

loveyourchurchseries.com

ACKNOWLEDGMENTS

Writing this book was an exercise in gratitude as it allowed me to reflect on the way God in heaven has welcomed me, and the ways he enables his saints to welcome others. To be a part of the body of Christ is an astounding gift.

I am grateful to both Acts 29 and The Good Book Company for inviting me to contribute this book to the Love Your Church series. What a joy to be spurred on by the other authors in this series. May these books honor the Lord and serve the reader. I am especially grateful to Christy Britton, who cheers me on personally and serves countless others professionally. Christy, thank you for sacrificially serving day in and day out, for your humor and enthusiasm, and for your excellent work. I am also indebted to Rachel Jones, my editor. Thank you, Rachel, for your care with my words and the message of this book. The whole church benefits from your skill and labor.

Many pastors and missionaries around the world took time to talk to me about this book. I have seen their creativity, compassion, and example in welcoming others into their faith families for decades. Brothers and sisters, thank you for laying yourselves down that others may know Christ and join his family. To the church planters around the globe, may you daily experience the abiding welcome of Jesus as you persevere in your welcoming work.

Redemption Parker, you are one the greatest and most unexpected gifts of my life. I am humbled to be one of you. I see the way you consistently open your homes, hearts, and lives to others. Your sacrificial and outward focus is no small gift from God. I thank the Lord for our elders, Gospel Community leaders, and faithful, ordinary saints who make up our beautiful family. And what a gift to have my nuclear family wrapped up in my faith family—Oshmans, you welcome others with great love, and I wouldn't want to do ministry without you.

Finally, I owe my life, my gratitude, and all my work and words to Jesus, who stopped at nothing to make me his own.

LOVE YOUR CHURCH

BIBLICAL | RELEVANT | ACCESSIBLE

At The Good Book Company, we are dedicated to helping Christians and local churches grow. We believe that God's growth process always starts with hearing clearly what he has said to us through his timeless word—the Bible.

Ever since we opened our doors in 1991, we have been striving to produce Bible-based resources that bring glory to God. We have grown to become an international provider of user-friendly resources to the Christian community, with believers of all backgrounds and denominations using our books, Bible studies, devotionals, evangelistic resources, and DVD-based courses.

We want to equip ordinary Christians to live for Christ day by day, and churches to grow in their knowledge of God, their love for one another, and the effectiveness of their outreach.

Call us for a discussion of your needs or visit one of our local websites for more information on the resources and services we provide.

Your friends at The Good Book Company

thegoodbook.com | thegoodbook.co.uk
thegoodbook.com.au | thegoodbook.co.nz
thegoodbook.co.in